ARCHIVE FOR OUR TIMES

To Carol
with love, respect
and enduring.
friendship
Bernice

ARCHIVE
FOR OUR TIMES

Previously Uncollected and
Unpublished Poems of
Dorothy Livesay

Selected and Edited by
Dean J. Irvine

ARSENAL PULP PRESS
Vancouver

ARCHIVE FOR OUR TIMES
Poems copyright © the Estate of Dorothy Livesay
Editorial postscript, notes, and indices copyright © 1998 Dean J. Irvine
Foreword copyright © 1998 Miriam Waddington
Afterword copyright © 1998 Di Brandt

ARSENAL PULP PRESS
103-1014 Homer Street
Vancouver, B.C.
Canada v6b 2w9
www.arsenalpulp.com

The publisher gratefully acknowledges the support of the Canada Council of the Arts for its publishing program, as well as the support of the Book Publishing Industry Development Program, and the B.C. Arts Council.

Poems reprinted with the kind permission of the Department of Archives and Special Collections, Elizabeth Dafoe Library, University of Manitoba, and the Bruce Peel Special Collections, University of Alberta Library, where applicable.

Cover and interior photographs reprinted with the permission of the Department of Archives and Special Collections, Elizabeth Dafoe Library, University of Manitoba.

"But We Rhyme in Heaven" by P.K. Page reprinted with permission from *The Hidden Room: Collected Poems, Volume 2,* published by The Porcupine's Quill, 1997.

Printed and bound in Canada

CANADIAN CATALOGUING IN PUBLICATION DATA:

Livesay, Dorothy, 1909-1996.
    Archive for our times

    Includes index.
    ISBN 1-55152-059-1

    I. Irvine, Dean J. (Dean Jay)   II. Title.
    PS8523.I82A85 1998   c811'.54   c98-910877-5
    PR9199.3.L56A85 1998

CONTENTS

ACKNOWLEDGEMENTS

To Dorothy Livesay's literary executor, Jay Stewart, for her cooperation in arranging and clarifiying legal matters; for her encouragement of this book; and for her permission to use published Livesay material.

To Miriam Waddington, for her Foreword, and for her generous thoughts on Dorothy Livesay.

To Di Brandt, for her Afterword, and for her perspicacious comments on my editorial practice.

To P.K. Page, for contributing her poem, "But We Rhyme in Heaven," for her supportive comments on the manuscript, and for priceless conversations over the years.

To Blaine Kyllo and Brian Lam at Arsenal Pulp Press for supporting this project from the onset; to Tamara Bates for ensuring that I actually reached Dorval Airport; to Kathryn Prince for making me believe that Dorothy Livesay deposited her papers at the University of Manitoba for so many unforeseen reasons; to Russ Bugera and Shona Hughes, and Russ Rickey, for hosting me in high style for my two research trips to Winnipeg in the summer of 1997; to Tim Conley for his couch and cuisine during my research trip to Kingston in the icy winter of 1998; to Lynn and Betty Holmes for graciously opening their home to me while I researched in Toronto during the spring of 1997 and summer of 1998; to Heather Fitzgerald for her long term and long distance support of my academic life; to Doug Beardsley for long talks in his garden and for enabling me to meet Dorothy Livesay in the summer of 1992; to Brian Trehearne for his academic and editorial advice, his careful study and inspired teaching of Canadian literature, and his contagious enthusiasm for archives; to Melanie Mortensen for shooting and developing photographs; to Chris Holmes for his untiring ear and insightful suggestions after reading the manuscript at a crucial time; to my parents, Ray and Helen Irvine, for everything, but especially now for having me back in Victoria during the most arduous stages of preparing the manuscript.

To Richard Bennett and his staff at the University of Manitoba Department of Archives and Special Collections for their solicitude and extensive assistance with their Livesay collection; to John Charles of the Bruce Peel Special Collections Library at the University of Alberta; to George F. Henderson at Queen's University Archives for allowing me to spend so many extra hours with their Livesay collection; to Henri Pilon at Trinity College Archives for locating rare issues of *St. Hilda's Chronicle*; to the staff at the Robarts and Thomas Fisher Rare Books Libraries at the University of Toronto for procuring copies and microfilms of periodicals; to the staff at the University of Victoria Archives for retrieving materials from their Livesay collection; to the McLennan-Redpath Interlibrary Loans staff at McGill University for rapidly processing so many last-minute requests.

The McGill Centre for Teaching and Research on Women deserves my gratitude for a Margaret Gillett Graduate Research Scholarship in the summer of 1997. I wish to acknowledge their gracious financial support and invitation to present a paper on my archival research in the fall of 1997. I also owe thanks to the Social Sciences and Humanities Research Council of Canada for a doctoral fellowship to continue my archival research in 1998-99.

As well, I would like to thank the McGill Institute for the Study of Canada for inviting me to present a paper on editing Dorothy Livesay's unpublished and uncollected poems at a conference in the spring of 1998.

Permission to quote from Elizabeth Varley's letters has been kindly granted by her daughter, Zanetta Varley. Acknowledgements are due for poems previousy published in periodicals, listed individually in the Chronological Index of Archival and Periodical Sources. I also gratefully acknowledge the permission of the following university archives and libraries to publish Livesay materials from their holdings: the Bruce Peel Special Collections Library, University of Alberta; and the Department of Archives and Special Collections, Elizabeth Dafoe Library, University of Manitoba.

—DEAN J. IRVINE

FOREWORD

by Miriam Waddington

I first met Dorothy Livesay in 1941 or '42. Before that we had met only in each other's poems which were published in Alan Crawley's *Contemporary Verse* on the west coast. Dee, as we called her, knew the Crawleys and was one of the founders of *Contemporary Verse*. (Floris McLaren, Doris Ferne, and Anne Marriott, also west coast poets, were also founders.) When Dee came to Toronto to visit her parents in Clarkson, she looked us up—that is, Patrick, my husband, and myself. That was the beginning of a friendship and correspondence that lasted up to her death in December 1996.

During all the years I knew her, poetry was the most important thing in Dee's life. She wrote prolifically and constantly in spite of the fact that she had a husband and two children. Her themes flowed from her daily life and her deep emotional interest in politics. But perhaps it was not politics so much as a hunger for justice and freedom in the world.

After we met Dee went back to Vancouver. We sent each other our poems hot off our typewriters, and we each responded enthusiastically, analytically, and critically. I have to laugh now when I read my own very serious written responses. (I have copies of my letters to her, but hers to me are scattered in libraries all over Canada.)

Apart from the books she authored Dee wrote many poems that were never published during her lifetime. Every poet has such unpublished poems somewhere in the back of a drawer. Sometimes poems are put aside until there is more time to finish them. Often that time never comes and those poems are orphaned and abandoned forever. Other times poems are put aside because they do not work, do not feel quite right to the poet, and so they are never really finished.

The group of hitherto uncollected and unpublished poems in this book has been lovingly collected by Dean J. Irvine. They aren't intended to be Dee's *best* poems, but they *are* poems, and as such must not be left out of the body of Dee's work. Scholars and researchers

9

will tell us about the *process* of making a poem. Moreover these poems reflect not just any process, but the particular process that engaged Dee.

They are presented here to Dee's readers. The thoughtful as well as the casual ones. One way or another they fell between the cracks of Dee's busy life as a mother, wife, and friend. They are presented here for the analysis of the serious student, as well as the pleasure of the most casual reader. More importantly, they form a part of the magical whole and the intimate tapestry of Dee's life and work.

In some mysterious way they are what Henry James referred to as "the figure in the carpet," and what we may call the invisible connective tissue between life and work. There are messages here: messages from the dead, still unrevealed. They are waiting for readers to decipher them, to bring them to new life and to discover their deeper meaning.

— MIRIAM WADDINGTON
Vancouver
August 1998

But We Rhyme in Heaven
For Dorothy Livesay—d. 1996

It is true. We shall. We do.
But earth is a briar patch—
one we never get through.
The moment we meet
tangles and snares spring up
on the asphalt street.
At airports and theatres
magnets pull us together
and we go for each other.

It is so irrational.
What is the bloody bone
we struggle and fight for?
Not my bone. Not hers.
An astrological quirk?
Or grit in the oil of the works
that set us in motion—some
meddlesome tamperer's mischief?
No part of us.

But her anguished, defiant phrase—
'we rhyme in heaven!'
is like a balloon
that carries our anger up
to a rarefied air
where rancour is blown away,
and remedial stars appear,
and Venus is kissing the moon
as the Spanish say.

— P.K. PAGE

IN HER CUPBOARD:
THE 1920S

It was years and years
Before I found the shoes there,
Still waiting.

Sleep

My dog is very still today
His paws limply crossed,
He gazes with dark, unfathomable eyes
Across the far valley flaked in mist
He might be a Buddha
Thinking—in the eyes of his worshippers—
Deep mystic thoughts beyond their ordinary minds
But in reality he is drugged
In the solid stupidity
Of stone.

The Gardener

He has made a garden
And so his soul
Has deeper soil than ours
Strange flowers flame there
Shy, untamed young things
Lifting their heads in sunlight
But fading into silences
At dusk.

They are the unspoken words
He dreams about
As he turns the black earth
And plants his seeds;
They are what makes in him
A vast quietness
A stillness of growing things
A love for June and for September
And for all slow things
We never seem to hear.

Year after year
The seasons lift their wings
And fly like new-fledged birds
Strong in their youth;
And so, year after year,
He follows change
Watching his seedlings grow and bloom and die,
Knowing that there is only
A little laughter,
A little weeping,
And then the long, long sleep.

In Her Cupboard

In her cupboard
A pair of shoes sat on their haunches,
Crinkling up their toes
In dumb expectancy
For morning.

But something happened
And her feet forgot
To put on their faces—
It was years and years
Before I found the shoes there,
Still waiting.

He Who Is Blind

i

Slowly the days walk by
For one who listens:
Even the minutes drop slowly
As water on stone
Leaving only a faint hollow
After centuries.

There is no sound
Save the dull sound of water dripping,
Clocks talking,
And the whirling, singing sound
Of atoms in the air.

✧　✧　✧

Now shadows rise and fall
Before my eyes.
Now there is a beating of wings.
Wings? Whose wings?
Wings that mock,
That evade,
That run and leap
And laugh with rustling laughter
In the dark.
Wings that I cannot see.
But only hear—
Wings that are gone.

ii

Quiet; all is quiet again;
It is black,
Black:
The wings, the shadows, have passed
And I hear
Only the minutes drop,
Water on stone.

The Priest

It was strange, the way it happened.
The nuns were fluttering back and forth,
Restless as birds.
It seemed
As if they would never be still,
Could never be still:
They were eternity itself
Yet he only had to stand:
He had only to move his hand
And soundlessly
The black shadows slipped
Through the door.

Down the gold length of the room,
He summoned me.
There was nothing left in the universe
Save my desire to go.
Yet when I stood near, with folded hands,
I did not know.
My heart stirred faintly,
As a child in the womb,
But I had not guessed.

There was silence.
And again, silence.
I saw his face,
Stern, remote, beautiful.
I was not afraid:
But when I saw his eyes
My soul was suddenly
Consumed with fire.

The words were on his lips
And I could not raise my hand . . .
He spoke . . .
The world wheeled, soared, sank.
I was alone with him,
Alone
Trembling.

It seemed
As if the moment would never pass:
As if we must stay there forever.
Impotent,
Holding our treasure close
Lest it should fall.
Lest it should fall.

But time passed.
The sunlight, stretched in a golden web
Around us
Suddenly broke.
My heat died down:
And in the darkness I passed him
With bowed head
Down the long, cold room
And out into anguished silence
Through the door.
It was night.

Meditations of a Thief

Now everyone is going to bed:
Shadows pass and repass the windows.
Why does no one think
Of pulling down a blind or two?
That woman now, with the fat arms,
Does she think her nakedness
As the young moon?
She must, else why should she pirouette
A mad imitation
Of the moon's walk?

Men, of course, can afford to be careless.
There is nothing ugly
About a man undressing
Except that he is so deliberately
Slow.
Women waste time
In vanity;
But men waste time
Making every moment
Have a meaning—
Socks here, braces there—
And so on
To infinity.

✧   ✧   ✧

The lights in the house I am watching
Have suddenly gone out.
But I must remember
That it takes some time to pray,
Think over the day,
Worry about tomorrow
And slowly curl into one's favourite position
For sleep.

Not all people sleep at once.
But that vain woman,
I know
Has gone off immediately
For she has no thoughts in her head.
Women are easy prey
Always afraid at the stupidest moments
And gloriously unaware
When danger is near.

I shall go out at once into this house.
It is too easy.
But I must be careful
Not to laugh aloud
For women are more afraid of laughter
Than anything else:
I have known it to break through their slumber—
And then, a shrieking woman
Is more terrible
Than a lion . . .

Transcendence

There is too much music.
I say it.
If I could cry, "Go!"
It should be.
Yet there are no words
Proud, triumphant—
Only a tumult of mad singing birds
Overwhelming whatever I might have remembered
Of words.

Hokku

Stoic?
I don't believe it.

A fine disguise, my friend,
For egoism.

The Butcher, the Baker, the Candlestickmaker

i

A stout man is he
Thick-fleshed as the meat he lays out on the counter
In the mornings, early.
Taciturn, not unkindly
He gives his wife orders.
She has a pleasant voice over the telephone:
He, a curt growl.
They have no children
And so their rooms, behind the store
Are polished and stiff,
Frigid and sanitary as a large white ice-box.
He is an excellent citizen
Who votes with passionate regularity.

ii

Next door to them, in his irony,
The Lord has placed a baker
With unnumbered children
And a whining wife,
But he is cheerful, benign,
White as his own pies.
He loves to wear a cook's cap,
For he is English:

His small spectacles
Twinkle
As he gives his opinions.
He likes beer, customers and Canada:
He never stays long in one place.

iii

Here is a man, an artist in his own way.
He is short, bent, with long, delicate fingers.
He does picture-framing, chiefly,
But behind, in secret, within a little room,
He is a potter.
Candlesticks? Perhaps, some few
In odd ingenious shapes;
And little bowls, carved, so it seems,
With fishes, prehistoric birds, a petal or two.
He lives alone.
On Saturday nights, late, he closes up shop
And steals out quietly, eagerly,
Into the streets.
Not, as you once supposed,
To satisfy desire,
But to watch the hurrying faces
Preoccupied, sorry, or glad
That stream along under the lights:
To gaze also into his neighbour's flashy windows,
To end up buying a sausage roll,
Or a meat pie
From his very good friend the baker.
In the morning he will be up early
Eager to take a Sunday walk
Into the quiet countryside.

Sudden Awakening

Out of the night—
Wind:
Out of the storm—
Rain:
Out of desire—
This flower, grief:
And so
To sleep again.

Emily Dickinson: Poet

No portrait of her face
Is left
Only, by some strange grace,
Were words forgotten, as she ran
To the Appointed Place.

The Woman Who Lived Alone

The sea is hungry for my garden;
The sea is gnawing at the rocks,
Burrowing in the sand,
Stretching out his arms
To hold my gaunt, salt flowers in his hands.

Sometimes I feed the sea
With faded petals
And old grey stalks
Nearly dead.
Poppies I fling him,
Scarlet and white,
And a few small roses,
Dying pioneers.

But the sea is insatiable,
He is always coming nearer and nearer,
Burrowing in the sand,
Gnawing at the rocks.

The sea is hungry for my garden,
And I am craving for the sea.

She Justifies Herself

I have sung many times of silence
Seeming to seek
That it is justified
By the song that breaks it.
What is the worth of silence
If no song comes after?
Yet, whether word or song follow
Wit or laughter,
Still I remember (going my sober road)
How it is after silence that the heart
Needs silence most.

From Shadow to Shadow

One eye winking in the sky
The lightning seemed—
Winking in—and out.
The frogs in the meadows below
Grinded their tune
(A rusty wheel going around in their mouths)
So we knew
That from somewhere the rain was coming.
Still the stars, scattered, distant
Hung in their places;
Not a breath disturbed
The delicate droop of a pine tree's arm.

Somewhere the rain was falling.

It was too warm to go in,
We said,
And too still to wander without.
We stood in the doorway and gazed.

—On a night like this, I said,
Stumps become crouching animals,
Trees become men.

—How is it, you mused,
That we compare things to men
Never men to things?

—Men are too assertive
Ever to borrow
An inferior image.
But you take a woman:
A man will not hesitate
To call her a tree or a cloud.
There are moments
When he hates to think of her as flesh only,
Like himself;
He identifies her
With a thing he can never realize . . .

—Yes, when I first knew you,
You were to me as remote and strange
As a cloud or a tree.
Now, knowing you better,
I would not for the world
Have you other than I.

—You are deceived,
For I am not you.
I am I
Which is an image . . .

—Don't let us talk.
Just listen to the frogs . . .
There, they've stopped
Suddenly.
Somewhere there is rain falling.

I turned,
And went into the house.
You stood alone listening,
For somewhere the rain was falling.

The Challenge

And I sitting here crouched
In the dark
Am aware of things you dare not name
Even when tightly shut within your room.

I sitting here crouched
Am one with fire
And one, too, with the earth
Where all fire falls.
I am of these, the element
You blind yourself against.

The Portraits

What did they know, those old men smiling,
Smiling and satisfied—
Those grandfathers?
What did they know, so quietly content,
That I know not?

Not the relentless morning, surely,
That tortures with the old taunt,
Urges the old uncertain quest
Into long hours of afternoon;
Not the swift tempest in the heart
That stings with desire and pain;
Not the wild young laughter, not the ecstacy—
Surely it is not these they knew,
Those old men, smiling:
Some other urgent secrecy is theirs
That they can sit so still
Beneath my restless look.

Accident

The road trailed into the river; one rough track
Fell away from the other and became
A grass-grown patch up to the riverbank—
Then over, a brief plunge through mud and stones
Until the water swallowed it in deep
Fast-flowing currents sucking down
Through multitudinous pathways to the lake.

Instead of stopping short in the grassy field
That edged the riverbank, it was not odd
(Lizzie had said), to run a car through the dark
Along what seemed merely a dark rough road:
And then, before you could put on the brakes, to plunge
Headlong into the river. (Lizzie had seen them go)—
Not many roads ended so stupidly.
It was not strange the car had tumbled so.
(Lizzie said it in court.) If Government
Could let such roads exist, well, accidents
Would happen on dark, sullen, rainy nights:
If such things were in spring, so much the worse.
No one caught in the floods could hope to live.

Her argument was right: it sounded right.
The inquest past, Lizzie would sit alone,
Boney and upright in her rocking chair,
Reading the papers; knowing them by heart.
"The only witness, Miss Elizabeth Gates,
Was standing alone at her door" (she was always alone),
"When out in the night and the rain she saw the lights
Fluttering on the road. It ended there,
In the field by her house. Before she could move at all
(Into the windy dripping dark), the car
Shot out into the path; and followed it
To the edge, and over"—"Yes, she had seen it go."
"And that was all?" They peered at her, the judge,
The lawyers, doctors and the grinning clerks.
"All." (For she was the only one there to see.)
"You had never known them before?" "Never at all."

(No one but Lizzie had seen them plunge and fall.)
"You think there were two in the car?" "I saw no more."
(It might have been one, they were lying together so close—
But nobody needed to know, since the bodies found
Were two, two lifted out of the river's drift.)
"You have nothing to say beyond that?" "That's what I saw."
(She had seen no more at the river's edge.
It was her affair, what she had seen before.)
"Very well. You may go." Someone had said it.
No one again would ask any further questions.
The pair were given a decent burial.

Lizzie returned, and sat by the river's edge.

It was queer, the urge that had sent her out,
Shivering, into that early, dripping dusk.
Sunday evening, and Lizzie tramping the road
In an old coat, with her limp grey hair all blown
Back wet from her face, and her gaunt arms swinging.
She passed the car on the road, going and coming.
Going she hardly glanced back—didn't she know
Without needing to look, what the couple were doing?
But coming back—above the sob of rain in the trees
She could hear the girl crying, sobbing and suddenly crying.
Lizzie drew near. It wasn't her business of course,
But still—"You will not go—not while I live!"

That was the man, shouting into the dark.
The girl kept crying. Lizzie stood still,
Wondering . . . They did not see her at all,
Huddled so close in the dark, and the girl crying.
"You brute!" It was Lizzie who heard her say it.
Then the wind swept down, scattering words like rain.

Lizzie went on. It was none of her business at all.
She went back into her house, and opened the door
At the side, so the wind could blow through the rooms.
She sat down and ate her meal, with only a lamp
To give her light. (The electric current was off.)
And when she had done she rose and stood
At the door, rain beating against her face, while the wind
Moaned through the dark winged trees.

                                    Along the road
Dimly a light flashed, moved in a mist
Of rain. Lizzie stood wondering.
"Not while I live!" he had cried . . . Why should they come
So far down a muddy road that only led
Into a field beside a tiny house?
The wind swept raindrops down over the bank
Into the roaring river. And she could not see
How near the car lights were, they flickered so—
Till, at a bound, they shot out into the field,
And above the drip of the rain a girl's sharp cry
Shook the air. The car shook, too, and reeled
And tumbled down. Then the river found them.

Lizzie stood braced at her door with the lamp behind her,
Her lips tight in a triumphing secretive line.

The Return

The earth is wounded with the noise of towns—
Her heart that knew the dream of quietness,
The lazy breath of sunbound afternoons
Unfolding into silence, now is stricken dumb
With sound. Take the axe's chime,
Clear metal striking into virgin sap;
And then the fall of trees, a sigh like swords
Withdrawn from silver sheaves. And following
Came horses with more metal in their wake,
The iron plough for stirring up the land.
Till houses grew there (where the trees had been)
And for a thousand years, perhaps, lived on
As quiet as the trees with wind in them.

—A flash of lightning and a thunderstorm!
Out of the air an iron giant rose
And clashed his cymbals with triumphant tread
And forced his music to corrupt men's hands,
Tearing machines out of their feeble grasp.

And still the trees, left standing in a park
Encamped and waiting for the enemy
Whose alien trumpets sound out through the night
To set the drooping leaves a-quivering.
So early scarred there with the constant jar
Of incoherent and persistent sound,
What wonder they are starved as any waif
Pale-faced and nervous, who has sprung up too
With these, in hunger, fearing injury.

What wonder then, that earth awaits her sleep,
Whose children know no place; the earth awaits
Returning mysteries—the fall of sunsets
On a barren land; cries of lonely birds
Like arrows shot from silence; the slow wheel
Of day and night returning without change
Over the young green grass or withered leaf.
These she will know, as old men know the sleep
Of after-living; as they stir and bend
Before a fire, before the children's shouts,
Aware of something waiting at the door.

Before the strident cries of crawling towns,
The ugly mouthing from the traffic's maw,
Old earth hears silence slipping up the street.

Where Is It?

Reader, if you are curious
To find in this book my proper self,
Warning! I, like the pepper-pot
Live each day on a different shelf.

INVITATION TO SILENCE:

THE 1930S

Sit still and be quiet just a minute, just a minute
All you befuddled poets and prophets
All you convinced of decadence, unable
To explain the stretched emptiness across the heart.
Words! I am ashamed to use words, you have so abused them
They were lovely once: now they have been corrupted
Crushed under the weight of too many meanings.
Yet I must use words, to make you listen—
You have only your ears left: your eyes are blinded.

Lazarus

The dark held me, Martha. Nay, weep not:
I am returned. Your laughter is a song,
Mary: I can hear. Even the bees
In their slow heavy humming, I can hear
As a great music after silence—so sudden
Your laugh is like a sudden waterfall.
I see the ribboned sun with aching eyes
And guess that this is summer overhead.
Silence lay with me, sisters. As a dream
She covered me. I was caressed, and knew
No more the tortured pain of mortal sleep,
And saw no more the mortal dark come down—
Only a shaken veil, a sleepy haze
Before that other dark, that seals the heart.

Yet still my ghost hung near, and could not rise.
My body lay as dead and yet the spirit watched
And could not struggle up into the light.
I thought: this is the price that I must pay
For quitting life too eagerly, before
I have lived more than half the allotted time
With only half the sorrow known,
Paid for. On earth I used to watch the joy and dream
Felicity was in the swallow's flight
And never pitied ghosts (as others do)
Who wander careless in the upper air.
But in the tomb my wings arrested there
Taught me the agony of spirits bound
To pass eternity between two worlds.
I was of these, who never could be free
Because on earth they lacked courageous faith
To tread the highest way, and lacked the might
For evil, and I was of these, most miserable
Three days on timeless wings, within the tomb
Sleeping and waking, as through eternal years
I waited dumb; until the wonder came—
Deliverance, I thought it meant, to heaven.
A burning light was in my eyes, I rose

And stumbled in the winding sheet, alone.
To heaven's gate: and there I saw
No angel, but your face, Mary. No street
Of gold, instead the ribboned sun
Upon green grass, the summer overhead
And men who cried: Lazarus walks, is wakened from the dead!

Was it my fault I smiled not, did not laugh
And weep with you? Martha and Mary mine?
All I could do was look into the eyes
Of him who summoned me, and understand
The sorrow and the kindness of his look:
All I could know, was how my way was not
To be a householder and brother now.
The desert and the wilderness, the road
Unending, hard; the agony of speech,
The loneliness of cities and of men.
The solitude amidst the heart of things
I saw in one brief look, and these I knew
Martha and Mary, where the other half
Of earthly years would lead me to.

So for a little while I stay at home
To quiet your strange fears, Martha.
Your tears, Mary; in a little while
I shall set out with an exultant heart.

Another Spring

Never before had I been out
Just at that moment of time, in the spring.
Never before had I caught
The amber willows as they were breaking
Into yellow leaf.
Like an old-fashioned broom
Making patterns in all directions
The willow trees swept the sky
And dusted the wind.
So then I sang and laughed
This loveliness being new to me:
But all the while the old sorrow underneath,
And I, wordless.

Yesterday's Children: A Cycle of Love Poems

To stand in sunlight is an easy thing
When all is well. The heart folds outward then,
A flower opening; and swift the sun
Leaves his mark graven there, for night to find,
For night to lay caressing fingers on.
But other sunlight have I known, when all
The heart within was dark, its petals closed—
Because the room wherein I stood alone
Lay dark behind me; there were waxen flowers
Instead of live ones, on the *étagère*;
And something not quite real, but made of wax
That let the breath through slowly, lay as still,
Unconscious of the golden afternoon.

To be alive, and strong; to feel the sun
When other part of you is lying stretched
In sick oblivion upon a bed:
No other pain so helpless comes as this—
The sudden double vision then of both
The life and death; which pass in Indian file
On other days— stealthily but separate.

✧   ✧   ✧

You are my sun: not fire that strikes and sears,
Not wind that sweeps away the tree, the leaf
And shapes the flower to his gaunt desire.
You are my sun, that warms me where I grow,
That draws me upward into the light—the blue
Of heaven fleeced with summer clouds.
I have no fear. You are not the rain, whom thirst desires,
But who is servant to the mighty wind
And so not trustworthy. You are my sun
That burns with silent fire, that walks the day
As a strong god who will not trample down
The little lives, the grasses in his way
But leaves them eager to pursue his step—
Like these I tremble, when your touch has gone.

✧ ✧ ✧

Don't criticize me while the blood is hot—
Nor analyse the phrase—
The passion there and not mixed metaphors
Will point my ways
Of loving you, of fashioning words too,
Of running out the days.

(This thought I murmured in the Tuileries
That Sunday afternoon
When children like the fountain-spray were blown
To the harsh tune
Of a down-bearing wind that snatched the leaves
And scattered them too soon.)

This is October; and my flaming month.
Be not harsh with fall
Of apples having had their russet day;
Or with the small
Bare look of once wide deepening woods,
Or with a last crow's call.

Be not too hard on aftermaths of love
When you will have the right
To meditate the things I said and did
And separate
Good fruit from false . . . Take now this moment's gift
Upon its flight—

Your hands be stirred and warm within its leaping light!

✧ ✧ ✧

I felt a hard and upright thing
Within me, till you came;
I was a flying bar, a stalwart stone,
With you opposed, the same,

Until I knew you love, and felt
Your bones like quicksilver
As sun upon chill snow beneath
Until the earth lay bare

And every quiver of yourself
Melted into me—
The ground released, we two arose
One inter-rooted tree.

✧ ✧ ✧

Break out, Heart, from the old metre
From the jingle
The self-sorrow.
Tomorrow shouldn't rhyme with that word
Anymore.

Tomorrow luminous
Inevitable
At peace
Tomorrow and the turning out of lights
Dark tomorrow nights, palpitating
Hard wakefulness dissolving
Into sleep.

No matter what I say—
How old it be—
Let me whisper it the new way
Softly
Or in sunlight, let me shout it
But cut out the jingle, the frayed endings
Syncopate the accustomed bang
Into a little trailing off
Chuckle.

Broadcast from Berlin

Do you see them running?—Who?—The workers.
Brownshirts striking out at flint,
Meeting flying sparks. The workers run to cover,
The workers dart behind their doors and stand
Fist clenched and eyes aflame.
The workers are as steel. Labour has made them
Strong and of great endurance. Toil has demanded
Sinew and muscle, steady, mighty heart.

The workers are as flint. The baton and the iron heel
Meet sparks. Arbitrary bonds are made by the swastika
But the people has its bond more strong, more deep
Of labour in the mines, of labour at machines,
Of labour in the smelting furnaces.
The many coloured shirts join hands. But long before,
The hands and hearts of workers had been forged.

Eagles and mystic symbols have no place
When men in every land together know
(As one together, understand)
The hammer's swing, the sickle's harvesting.

Look to the end! Look to the strength in us,
Look to the stride already made and held.
You see the workers run. But see instead
The work behind closed doors, the unity
Of purpose in our silent searching glance.
Friend? Or enemy? Each worker knows his brother,
Your fight is our fight, your struggle our success.
Workers of the world, we have grown up at last,
At last we face the answer we have sought!
Our people are in line: across the world it holds,
It surges forward. It is the very storm,
A storm of labour, tearing up old roots,
Bringing to the earth fresh nourishment.

Will you fall away? "No!" Millions echo back.
Onward comrades: for the spring is ours—
Within ourselves we hold
The harvest and the final reckoning.

Testament

We moved this way before; observed the leaves
Of restless poplars merging with bulrush spikes
The sun a haze drawing warm sweet odour
From the marsh and the marsh-wet ground.
Clothes without thinking we took off
To be free and relieved of thought
And after caressing, bodies together moving
We could withdraw released as the tree from the wind
Yet not divided, quiet in our escape
For a moment only: days folded away
Between hot asphalt and the tap, tap, tap
Of offices, their files, their rubber stamps
Days for a moment only remembered, held
In the mind while the nose was pressed
Against hot glass, the wary eyes aware
Of flat black roofs, a city's offering
To the sun and the far planets.

Business of living crushing us, until
We come out from between the rollers
Flat as newspapers, with a few headlines
For recognition, someone's photograph, and a "lost" column.

In the beginning, in the folded away
It was all sensation. Feel it, the air sings
The sun burns in exaltation.
Or here is dirt, ugliness, squalor
Children in rags with tear-smudged faces—
We recoil, at all costs brush out the memory.

When thought began to push a shy root
Into our consciousness, our sensitive crust,
Sensation took on new form—
An illustration of the indictment.
We know nothing, we haven't touched anything of living
We live in the sun, casting a shadow
On all the others, the nameless, the toilers
And our sun-life, untouched by shadow
Is not a life, is a scorched blade.
There must be a way out for those in the shadow:
Can we join them, can it be found?

Moving over then, with the masses
Afraid to touch, and be friendly,
Afraid to be found out, and jeered at:
"You—you came from the sun!"
Fear dwindles, in the growing knowledge
The growing oneness of work to be done.
We look at the sun, and are not blinded
The sun our attainment, and its parasites
Blades of burnt grass to be trampled.
Was it so once for us? Were we once so,
Parasites burnt with a false possession?

Returning now to the trees felt then, not known,
To the leaves and the bulrush spikes
Returning with understanding, we have delight
Because there is no longer isolation in the valley
We come not to the marsh seeking self-effacement
We come now with others to share this joy.

Look, we have secrets comradely yielded:
Here is the earth, rounded and warm to be taken:
And the wind for all city lovers and children
Is a banner upshaken.

Man Asleep

Though hunched in grass as mountain rocks take root
Hunched over towns, their contours blocked and blurred
Receding at the march of evening, mute—

Though unresisting while the summer's hand
Smooths out your brow, relaxes the stiff bone
And cools the blood—somewhere the guns command.

There, dreaming one, your brothers raise the dust
Over Madrid, gird the impassive hills,
Cast off mandragora with lightning thrust;

There, sleeper, do the men like clouds oppress:
Stiffer than yours, their bones, their feet
Footsore with battle, not with homelessness.

See, the world's home they build in Spain—
The fireside stone you never had, the arms
You snatched at, but could not maintain.

Now hunched in sleep you dream the battle's done:
But still your bones shall spring to life like steel
Clamp down on victory, behold the sun!

The Second Journey
(from a train, at night)

Locked in this berth
Rocked with this bone
My belly pressed against her ribs
Each sigh of hers my own

Swayed with these thighs
Sped on this gear
In a blind, dizzy world
Each minute a slow year:

Thus in your womb I lay
And now, this span,
Plunge to my destination—
Open eyes on man.

Invitation to Silence

Sit still and be quiet just a minute, just a minute
All you befuddled poets and prophets
All you convinced of decadence, unable
To explain the stretched emptiness across the heart.
Words! I am ashamed to use words, you have so abused them
They were lovely once: now they have been corrupted
Crushed under the weight of too many meanings.
Yet I must use words, to make you listen—
You have only your ears left: your eyes are blinded.

Sit still and be quiet just a minute, just a minute—
Forget the tinklings and the jangle: there is volume behind them.
A slow sound comes first, linked with a hot afternoon
When the stubble already reaped is a sunburnt copper
This is the sound of men steadily loading a wagon
Swiftly intense and throbbing as it nears the barn
Where the threshing machine repeats the cricket's staccato.
There is a silent cry behind this labourer:
"Wheat! Wheat! And no one to buy or eat
And yet we have heard that children cry and starve in the street."

Tap, tap, tap. Steel on rock. Steel in the darkness tapping coal.
The shaft and the mining town have their cry as well!
"If we slave in the dark, if we go down hungry
Must we return empty-handed to the women and children?
Shall we offer them coal to eat? Or shall we fall asleep
Remembering rather this struggle at Estevan
And three of us shot for demanding bread?
In the morning we will be readier still
To avenge Estevan; to struggle and organize!"
Tap, tap, tap: steel on rock. Steel in the darkness tapping coal.
Steel men in the earth, unbreakable, will send
Fuel for the factories.
Coal drawn from blood will not be burned without
Its meaning being borne to those who work,
Whirling the wheels, giving the vast machines their pace.
Their struggle is the same, they hold the cities in their hands.

You, who see the chimneys and the smoke,
The early whistles rousing you from sleep
As demon things—what is their power, save
As things men built? As things that only conquer man when he
Is slave himself to wealth's democracy?

Shake off, shake off your radio-trained ears
And hear the thunder of non-broadcast sounds.
Production makes the world. These men will be
Not Gods or prophets, but singers of this world.
To you, this century is chaos: but to them
Order and peace are harboured in its roar.

Someday if you sit still and listen, as I said
Your hearts may start to thump, an awful fear
Will set you gasping; you will be listening
And only your own heart will thump in answer.
You will be shouting and only your own voice will echo.
Someday silence will seize you; you'll hear silence:
Wave on wave the hushed drumming will surround you.
Silence from the ploughed lands, the sweet unruffled
Silence from the dark mines, the silver rail.
In the factories and workshops not a wheel will be turning
The still sky unshrouded by the least whisp of smoke.

Will you understand then, the meaning? Will you know
Why the world stopped? Perhaps you have a neighbour,
Perhaps he will tell you, whispering words slowly:
"I've heard of this before: it's general strike"—
The words mean nothing: the words are empty,
Empty as the sudden quiet world,
Until one word comes hurling, striking at the root of you,
Crumpling all the pettiness, turning rust to dust,
Until from the ploughed lands, the mines or the factories
"Revolution"'s sounded out in many marching feet.

In Praise of Evening

The excitement of evening, bare relief
In living, and thrusting the hand out
In taut silhouette against sunset
As a tree on the rim of horizon:
The liveness of breathing, clenched against hunger
Leaving defeat behind on the doorstep
The heart resilient with April's motion
Contracting, expanding to earth's own rhythm.
This will defend us from famine's gesture,
The run on the banks, panic at noonday,
Bones to a dog and taunts to a beggar,
Chattels and dishpans set on a sidewalk;
The will to be rooted, but like a tree waving
Sifting the air through boughs and branches
Leaning to lover, urgent with blossom
In wise embracing shielding the seed.

A Mother, 1918

Blue from uncertain skies
Can pierce the sense
Like periwinkle's brief
Star conversation in the grass.
In self-defence
I close myself to spring
Remembering your eyes.

That year the summons came
You went unwept
Unsung by anyone
Till smoke deflowered you, and drill
Of steel fang leapt;
The bomb, the snout uptore
Your roots, your body's frame.

O loveliness. O son
Whose eyes, flow'r-blue
They stole the colour from:
Let me be covering and gown
For girls you knew . . .
Let me alone face burnt-out eyes
Where love had flowers sown.

New Day

Let day be early, piercing the dome of eyelids,
Streets and memory swept with the night's rain
And pulse to pulse (footsteps against pavement)
Let bodies rise to dancing deeds again.

For we have passed by midnight with her slanting hips
Faced the leer and the thieves' challenge
Run amok in the dark of a gutter, heard
Unseen around the corner rout of war . . .

Now held steady by the stars' composure, we
Have taken breath again, the shock of sudden air
Like blow on blow rained at the body's pores
Has straightened out the limbs, prepared release.

Now day is early, summoning her bird songs,
Lovers of upland and of salt sea coves;
The broom will grow again, old sun's forerunner,
And hearts will leap like salmon to their loves.

At the Beach

Even the headlines break upon
Our seaward gaze
And from the funnelled smoke of ships
Words shape and blaze
Of exodus, of mass arrest
(Here, sunlight quivers on your breast).

Even the boom of waves' advance
Like thick-lipped guns
Licking their tongues upon the shore
A horde of huns
Hungry for prey, for sandy snare
For flowers of spray caught in your hair.

Even the lilting wind betrays
Where he has raced
Past stench of bodies stripped to bone
By bombers' haste—
Even our arms embracing here
Are split between love and fear.

SOS

Deet deet deet remorseless as rain
He hammers out the code, channelled in deep-sea pit,
The waters now assembling in a cloud
Formation, meeting in thunder grip—
A knife-slash on her deck, then slow ooze back
Followed by sprouting spray, a wreathe of hair
Shaped to a masthead, fastened to the prow.

Deet deet deet da da. The shriek
Of raw metallic language. Comrades here
Call help. Send greetings to green worlds.
Deet deet deet. The pumps. The captain says
If not next moment's puff, then looming NOW
Time nosing forward like an iceberg snout
Upon us! Only the women in the boats—
The operator's left above, the girl untorn
From grim assertion on the forward deck.
Now not to break or beat, up hand and heart
Da da deet deet quick quicker unity
Unless you court defeat and lick old sores
Reverse your engines! Set your compass here . . .

Too late. The splutter-spitting da-de-da
Is tattered rag and shattered SOS.
"Hold on" voice cried, "together here"—
Then waters licked her nostril's lip
With salt, and sprayed the foaming brain.
This sea invasion, barricading hordes
Flooded her passages: the signalling
Spluttered da da, alighted, stopped.

After, a scouting plane might spy
(Searching with gulls the empty sea)
A bloated face, dead messages
Curled carelessly in the wave's arm
Their meaning blotted out; might hear
The sea heave endlessly above the sound
Of rotting timbers, ship's bell clanging under sand.

Grouse Mountain

Seek you a source? The cold and the rain's abandonment
Spring from the same transparent heaven,
Usurp some essence from the sea's sparkle.
Fear neither to search the source, nor tremble
At stormy ravages en route, the river choked
With leaves and unprotesting broken trees—
Once the adventure's stamped in photograph
Upon your mind, no hesitation's brooked;
Leap there beyond hooked branches, clawing rocks,
Caress the tresses of a waterfall
And climb through shattering spray to pools above.
(O wayward wish, to reach the clouds in dream
Without these thorny scars, this ribbéd gash.)
And, panting on the earliest plateau
With windy mist outstripped,
Pause to consider how the fountains fall,
Into what brilliant green the fir trees march
Who but an hour ago cast shadows dank
As death. Lift wider eyes towards the overflow
Of light, on the crisp plains below: and gaze
Fulfilment's ease upon the sea's far face . . .

Here is your breathing-space between old earth
And older rocks: your rest from frenzy's cry:
Until the heart pulls upward and the snow's
White spirit summons you to where
The Lions muse in fierce repose together,
Challenge your presence in the sunlit air.

Spain

The rowan berries bunched in red grape clusters
Beckon like wine to birds who winter with us;
See how the tree has clenched her ripening fruit
As though a thousand fists were offering
Their tangible testimony to withstand
All winter's bullying blasts.

A little country on the map of Europe
Stands so, as firm
And in the clenching of her fists
A harvest yield is spread
For those who'll not take flight, but stay
And winter with us.

Lullaby 1938

Life for my kid
Is a hammock swinging
(Swing high, swing low)
The sorrow on the other side
Tomorrow will know,
The hunger in the ditches
Twenty years will show.

Bumping in a box car
Through prairie silence
(Sweet wind, sweet night)
Plunging from a tunnel
Into orange light—
Lined up on the pavements
Trapped from flight:

Life for my kid
Will be a baton swinging
(Swing high, swing low)
A welt across the shoulders
From the brutal blow
And a mark on the consciousness
Where fiery fruit will grow.

The Anarchist
(for Bob Bouchette, drowned June 13, 1938*)*

Cool cup of bay
Fern frosted—
Sand curled by waves—
Evergreens twitching winged shoulders
Blue clam shells in the tidal caves—

A body could be
Sheer song
Swinging there
In wave's hammock;
A song could be
As yours was
Child-song free of bondage.

But you rounded the point
End of green world's finger
And heaving high, grey world
Pushed iron shoreline sharp against
The curves, the melting bosom.
Back flowed water running fast
From the jutting jetty's thrust
Steamer's tail and stony tongues
Of street licking the docks.
Back foamed water blocking ears
From churn of engines; left instead
Of ferry's taunt and bronchial engine blast.
Silence chugging in the head.

Rearing now, proud skyline stood
On tottering stilts to top the other fellow,
Fierce ugly heads craned out and leered
In jabbering talk—this face
This city's crazy face . . .
Then high foamed water, stinging eyes
From sight of wall's collapsing smack
And chimneys' seaward fall—
Blotted out the floatsam voice

Flat cigarettes and spattered beer
There, on cleft corner of mock-marble floor:
Disintegration of an argument
Wave-washed from vision's door . . .

Outward and seaward ploughing now,
Deaf and blind
Finding sea eyes, new ears
In nostrils furrowed by the salt
Sob of the wind.
Sensing new company where night
Tossed away brightness
Poised and dived softly
Sea-enveloped . . .
Deep down diving
Within yet outside of
Sea's opalescent shadows thrust
By waves of darkness.
Within yet outside of
Body pulsing
Feeling the water's womb yet head above her:
Breast now the downing arms,
Beat back the salt-sprayed wind,
Fight and give battle!
Clutch at her mouth and swallow her foam
Thresh out with arms till her arms wrestling
Are curled in a cool clasp soothing the shoulder.

Quiet now, quiet. A lull and a rest time,
A sweet low breather on sea's crest rising.
Night now has lulled himself upon the horizon
And day says its last word to the pounding heart.

Quiet now, quiet. Till mind alert, easy,
Hand over hand striking mid-current
The bones turn over . . . shouting defiance
Meet the last wave with salmon's leaping
Hitting sky rim and mountain meeting
Then fall, go under, knife-deep downwards
To tunnelled channels, sea-green places
Downward and downward . . .

Far behind the heaving breast,
Night's shadow, flowers of sun or snow;
Downward and downward to the still room below
Where quiet water spills its circles,
Its pressure sounding, pounding slow.

Scourge

Dusk in the hushed wood.
Clouds of smoke, feverish
Festooning the tree trunks,
Furtive nostrils along the ground
Smelling out leaf-rusted hollows.
In the gullies a choked silence.
No one breathed.
Not a grass wavered.
Trees stood stalwart.

Now the wind, crashing
Tree against tree
Crowding the wood
With its loud pushing.
Partridge whirred by in thunder
Crows cackled and circled
A chipmunk scolded, the teeth of the wood
Chattering, chattering in the wind.

Crackled the flames
Hot wolf tongues, panting,
Insatiably licking the green sap of its victim
To the roar of falling armies
Giants hissing and sobbing
Tearing open the ground
As they crashed.

And now
Fire had reached the wood.
Hot from the scorched earth
Scuffling and rustling
Scurrying, jostling
In haste forgetting
Caution's warning
Swifter than fear
Run the wood's own creatures
Chipmunk and squirrel
Rabbit and deer

Crows down swooping
Partridge drumming
Scared thrush flapping
Through the underbrush.
And the cries of all
Of fur and feather
Muffled together as falling water
Slender bird trill, common scold
Crying in anguish, converging together
As faster and faster
With quick heart's hurry
They sought out the slope where poplar trees
Strained away from the wind.

Then the wind; the brazen flames.
A slashing butcher with knife of fire
Scorching the fur and singeing the feather
Sucking the throat and plucking the eyes—
Till the scream
The scream of blast furnaces rose
Gathered up steam and with bullying blows
Blast earth asunder.

The thunder overrode the sound
Of small alarms and little bodies downed;
Inferno seared the world and mountain high
Fire hit the sky . . .

Question

Who knows the needs of man?

Say that he came as a lover
Circling warm breasts with the ring of his mouth
Immemorial signet under summer stars.
Say as a songster and lover
A laughing gangster
He came to unlock the body
And it sufficed them.

Who knows the needs of man?

Say that he came for the mother
Cool and indifferent seeming
Polite always
Yet yearning for his head at rest
And a hand stroking the hair
Easy and uneasy one
Quick to go.

Who knows the needs of man?

Say that he was the father
Loving the guideship
Tending the plant in earth with garden fingers
Wise with sunlight—
Say that it suited them so
To keep love sleeping.

> *Who knows the needs*
> *Urgent, quiescent*
> *Easy, uneasy*
> *The willful and yearning*
> *Necessitous learning*
> *Of man and man?*

I, Challenger

Dancing in the heat to the tom tom beat
Of the sun, our forefather, our sap where branches run,
Raking in the heat and swaying low and lifting high
The hay sun-suckled like our children's skin
And sweet to breathe as wind when haying's done—
Dancing in the heat and lifted on a prong,
Shouldered in wagon-loads against the sky—
My throat was parched with sun and song, my arms
Raised love's small bouquet like a daisyful
In each ascending sheaf of sweetened grass.

There on horizons giant figures moved,
Behind the sun my shadow seared the world:
The horses, blunt and widely spread as clouds
Reared at their own disfigurement, in fear:
But I rejoiced, a shield for earth and sun,
In shadows marking out my claim and moving on . . .

Till thunder jarred horizon's calm, and clouds
Usurped my dancing pace. I, challenger,
Am challenged. As a knife bites to the heart
The sun is riven, blotted out, the air
Touches with sameness every fence and tree,
Merges these horses and their wagon-load.

And now what shaft of difference shoots between
The naked poverty of trees, the bare
Grass blade, the aching arms I lift
Into the rain-swept disenchanted air?
This rain will sweep, the prairie jettisoned,
And eyelids be pressed downwards like the leaves.
So levelled out with rain, living beneath its breath
We grow familiar with the pulse of stone
And patient as the crumbling yield of wood;
As shadowless as any hidden leaf
We yet absorb, moistened for early growth:
Sifted, but not for burial,
Clawed to the very root, but not for death.

Words for a Chorus

Who is she? The lady in your hearts,
The signal to your hopes?
She with the Beaver on her shoulder?

Her quick stride brings her to the centre of the wheatfields;
She stops to suage her cool hands in the rivers:
The Hochelaga Saint quivers and rolls eastward
While Fraser sweeps on southways, to the mellow coast.

Who is she, rain bringer from Belle Isle
Her eyes lake blue as blue unfrozen water
Scanning with firm glance
The farthest snow peak, the glacier jewels?

This is her frame, her outward kindness;
Her spirit moves in other quiet places.
You have seen her in the harsh voice of Pool County—
That farmer's wife, skimpy, her head an acorn,
Who shrills to the hand: "Go fetch the cattle."
And in the gaunt gaelic of Breton's island
You have seen her face in awe uplifted
At the strange bird-whirr of a monoplane.
She ploughs with the peasant women, head bekerchiefed
Through sun-burnt barrens and crocus flame;
She lies low in the saddle over copper foothills
And bears her child in an Okanagan orchard.
And last, in an endless chain you have seen her marching
Feet on fire from fierce contact with pavements
Marching, a restless seeker at iron gateways:
Offering her hand as antidote to hunger:
Marching and sometimes singing, then muted marching—
A thousand songs kept for another springtime . . .

And will they blossom?
Will fruit ripen to be gathered?
Will meals be ready on the supper table
And hymns arise from the weeping heart?

Who is she? The lady in your hearts,
The signal to your hopes?
What mercy bestowing
On hands upstretched and empty?
Who is she, who warns you to be ready,
Who rends your blindness with a searing fire?

War

The wide sweep of your living dwindles me
And my horizon to a hole in the wall
Room for no movement save the roaming eye's
And cat acquaintance with a gutter world.

You in your spring possess the greening leaf
The early leap from bed, the splashing song
As from a water-tap the fountain falls—
Inundate bliss, skin open to barrage.

And inwardly your mind takes broader scope
From its environment; a seaplane set
Amidst the fuzz of foam, but free to rise
And storm the volleys of the alien fire.

Compared with yours, my thoughts limp in their gait
And seem a feeble protest when the guns roar out.

2000 A.D.

Who will comprehend our silence, who today
Stifle the honest word?
Will you understand the gestures that were made
That fell unseen, unheard?
And laugh, O thousands
At weight of yoke and gird?

In earth's embowelled stillness, voices wait
For their appointed hour;
The sun's magnetic needle, piercing through
Encrusted leaf gone sour
Shall wake, O people
A dreaming giant's power!

We Are Alone

We are alone, who strove to be
Together in the high sun's weather.

We are bereft, as broods a tree
Whose leaves the river sucks forever.

We are as clouds, which merge and vanish
Leaving breathless the dead horizon—

We are as comrades, whose handshake only
Comes rare as leap-year and mistletoe morning.

Each one ploughing a one-man clearing
Neither one alive to see

In wider boundaries of daring
What the recompense might be.

Reply to a Time Server

Cover me with no shroud,
Offer me no death. I'll not be bribed
With glittering raiment, easy pass for heaven.
That you have fought with living men, caressed
Spain's totured body, cleansed her wound,
And now could turn her to a seducer's arms—
That is no argument for public flaunt.
Your logic is a lull in thought,
A tragic lapse of heart. I'll not resign
The task first recognized: necessity
To grow; living, to fight; no easy mark
Disaster can make mock of. And your words,
A treacherous treacle, will not dull my ears
Nor flail the resolution of my mind.

MOTIF FOR A MURAL:
THE 1940S

Bound in the bands of colour, burned
A salamander, I:
Or phoenix who
In worlds' own ashes lie

Hands

You would not know these hands, for they were poised
In bright precision, pointing to the shy,
Elusive wind, evoking worlds from phrases,
Eve's garden from a honey-suckle bell.
And they were birds, swift sailors on the rain,
The vanished cloud. And they breezed into storm
With gay abandon, spending easy vows
In rain and sunshine, veering with the weather.

You would not know them. Even you, who caught
And held them tightly in your shining palms;
Who soothed and fêted; laughed about and teased
Endearing no divinity where none had grown . . .

You would not know these hands—so cracked and worn,
At work at last, earth nurtured, travail torn.

Motif for a Mural

i

So many young men
Released into our streets
Shifted to low gear
Thrown in reverse.
So many young men
Hurry from silence
Wear on their brow
The brand of a brother.
So many young men
Run in their sleep
Resistless running
But walk in the street
Patient and cunning
Proud
Of the deeds unsung
Alone
With the unnamed name
Burning the tongue.

So many young men:
So many and young.

ii

In the time of speech
I came forward
Made speeches
The inert audience
Leaned spineless
On a column of words
Grandiose in a tower of strength
Loaned from a leader,
But liquid as water:
For the curtain fell
And the people melted.

In the time of action
I pranced on a black horse
And the crowd roared
The guns exhorted
Skyscrapers toppled
Cathedrals perished
In the mounting movement
The astounding action.

When the rubble was lifted
The black horse snorted
But his saddle was empty
The rider routed.

In the time of quiet
I lay under a stone
Weeping
And the grass grew again
Green in a gold oasis
And the well was watered.
In the time of quiet
No one listened
Nothing shouted:
And the world's infested
Wound found healing
Licked by tongue
Of the ancient sun.

iii

Now curl me colour, a plumed cloud
Purple to circle the sky!
And a blue shaft darted
Thought's charger mounted,
Drench me with orange, let fly
The burnt gold rain
The tropic sunshine shafted
Into a wheel of fire
Vaulting the monument, the spire
And on its shadowed side, dove grey

Luring the light to fold its wings
Against a scarlet day.

Now dash and daze me in the sway
Of yellow, gold and green
Rock me in a summer breeze
And set my swing between
The shift and shimmer of green leaves
Where sun's sharp fingers lean!

Bound in the bands of colour, burned
A salamander, I:
Or phoenix who
In worlds' own ashes lie:
Affirming the still firmament, the flame
Leaping to meet the master sun
Praising his fiery name!

Boy

Boy's born again each day!
Blind booms up and white
Clear light beats on the eye,
Startles the chair
To life, gives tongue to talk
To one-eyed teddy bear.

Somehow the dark got pushed away
Like blankets off a bed
Somehow Mr. Sun got up
And kicked his legs and said:
"I'll make it warm today."

He bluffs his way downstairs
Tooting a horn! and zoo-oom
He's down the hall, a truck
Dumping his load
("Any wood today?")
Or cr-rash! And his aeroplane
Busts into blazing flame.

And yesterday? Where's that?
Ah gone, in complete contempt,
Utter relinquishment. Only the grooves
Of tiny habits, deeper bitten-in
Each day, these survive to say
Where past hours went
And how was learning spent . . .

Today? Tomorrow? Puzzlement
No pause for long at barriers:
Turn back; back to the toy in hand
The work to do: "I'm helping you."
And: "See the yellow sun today?
He's laughing to me. Time to play."

The Take-Off

This early brood of breath-takers
Precariously poised for flight
Set out from the heart's four corners
Wind seeking, in airy pockets sailing,
Drifting to rockward, cloud spinning,
Over the ruèed water skirming.

This first brood of joy-takers
Sped with the soul's authority
Mind's blessing, children of bliss
Strike forth in growing strongness to the outer fastness
High fortress of sea and air, weapon armoured . . .

Their going is knowing
Their aim is being
Small loves homing in their hearts
And their destruction-loaded bombers
Bear the brunt for love:
There in sea light, ocean dazzle
There at sky's emblazoned roof
There the goal is: perched Disaster
And, principled in state
The high god of Hate.

Variations on a Theme by Thomas Hardy

i

O stranger with the arms outstretched
Lamenting rain drives in between
Today's demand, what might have been.

Eternal lover on the Cross
Reaches only with his voice
The lovely creature of his choice

And no summation even holds
Completion in its still embrace:
If of the flesh, the spirit's trace

Is gone; if spirit, there is never known
Burden of breath. Lamenting rain
Drives and separates the twain.

ii

And sunlight has a brittle snap
Even in spring. We walk the roadway of our dream
Together; but the willow's pace in wind
(Gathering gold on bough)
Is lonely, willow in wind
Is separate, sealed earthward, out of range.

iii

Eternal lover is the one
Who seeks no marriage of the bone

Borrows his raiment from the spring
Owns no roof, bestows no thing

With his insignia; more free
To range than willows be.

Eternal lover will not clutch,
But waits; waits the returning touch.

iv

"How is your bed so cold?"
"It lies by the outer wall."

"How are your limbs so rigid, then?"
"I have grown tall."

"Why is your heart so still?"
"It's tuned to upper air."

"Your eyes are icy stones."
"So do the stars stare."

"How was your breath blown out?"
"At lightning's pace."

"Where are you love . . . my love?"
"Look. In the sky's face."

Invasion

We hear no bomb scream through the unarmed wood
No flares search out the whippoorwill.
Springs from an unmolested soil, marsh wet
Suckle the kingcup and the violet.

We hear no bomb. We see no flare.
We sit no vigil on a stony stair
Expecting the dead child to stir.
Yet bombs fall here. And fires sear.

Flowers explode. Tomb's riven open
The mind surveys her many fallen,
Trees charred and pencilling the sky
Write a sign language for her eye.

Conception was. Heaved on a hasty bed
Clutching at high sensation, dubbed it love
And birth began, cracking the rigid bone
The room for innocence a vacant one.

Our mind our mother brooding in the night
Was prodigal, was spendthrift of her young.
Unnourished these: toddlers and strugglers
These her thoughts must battle all alone.

So the warped song, the music out of key
The picture painted without symmetry;
And now the mask, ripped from a naked face
The summer sickle stricken in its dance.

Shrill the bomb bursts. The flare falls.
On us. On you. We laid our mines long since.
The stifled whisper in the secret wood
Was known, was trumpeted far hence:
On sun-stained boughs, bird-mutilated morns
Harsh crackling music overrides, outwarns.

Letter from Home

If mired in foxhole or some moonless road
Mud sucking at boots, the Lowland wind
Sucking your heart: perhaps you hear
The news from home, the radio, or word
Flashed in lieu of torch: you know
Election's on, with midnight still
Holding taut faces to the radio.
Perhaps in a lonely space of night
Unburdened of all other men who be
Torn from you by the guns or the flak's sound
You go unbrothered, momentarily lone.

Maybe you know now what the struggle was,
And why you came away; why crackling leaves, bush smoke
Lights swaying on St. Catherine St.
Why these, marked with indelible delight,
Were boxed and put away
Child toys in cupboard, waiting for the day.

And if you call me now, I'll answer sure
Who in a maze of haste and hate
Let joy go by and the heart's gate
Swing to a swift close.
I will be ready with a mind
Swept clear, a heart free
From fear, foot sure
The new way fair and dear.

And though we be alone forevermore
And never meet on city street
And leave by a different door—
Your way is mine, mine yours
And the wide sea, the cloud-spent sky,
This heritage is ours!

Of Love

"I" is becoming, and "we" creating.
The racketeer shall meet his truth:
Stripped of his garment, in painful knowledge
Seeking himself he finds the other.

Day dissolves and ego vanishes
Into the womb, the new dominion:
Day dissolves but night's slow unison
Strived for and won, will never perish.

For Paul Robeson: Playing Othello

i

Illumination of the Word: O man
Emmanuel! Warming waves of sound
Fall through a sea of silences
Fall and resound.

Words lifted from our world's first tongue
Now penetrate, inform this voice
And from this voice a thousand times outflung
The echoing circles reach, embrace, rejoice!

> (As wind-combed, sandy beaches lie
> In fallow forms outstretched
> Laved by the leaping waves
> And by the watery pencil sketched
> In thousand shapes, disturbed, at rest,
> Vision impermanent
> But beaten upon the eye and ear
> A fossil element . . .)

ii

That faltering one, who looks not straight in eye
For fear of losing self's reflection there:
That brutal one, his glance an iron wall,
Lashes his tongue and violence topples all.
The lonely one, companioned by the crags
Of mountain morning, loving light
Yet fearing its swift flowering in a place
So humble as the human face—
And last, the simple soul, wizened in years
Yet wizard in the love he bears—
These feed upon his words. As young lambs from a fold
Serenely furl on grassy hill
These drink the sun spill, swallow vibrant air
Lose littleness, grow in the world they share.
These, given of beneficence
Learn to breathe its air
And as the mountain cherishes
Its children, they build mountains there.

iii

A song prevailing, sung through one
Who gives it noble bearing
Who dark of skin, sheds light of sun
Illuminates the word he's wearing.
The hand of man, tearing asunder
The pitiful mask his own hand wrought
Putting the hate aside to render
Love for murder; and in the hot
Wound, balm for pain:
Or set a kiss upon its stain . . .

O voice availing, crying now
Upon man's wilderness: Go, do thou!

Prairie Town

All angular you danced—
Egyptian style? No, far
From desert, but a desert place
Interminably straight, no curve to shoot,
No hills to struggle with
A gas tank for a Sphinx and Tigris here
Moved sluggish red; mirrored no sky . . .
Trees spindled out on boulevards
Naked in winter as a frozen hand
Snow-bound—life tombed below.
One knew no cutouts, copses, cool
Sequestered summers; and the cottonwoods
In country sheltering a marsh
Seemed unacquainted with those painted trees.
The only flower, bursting in powerful
Strong-scented, heady spring
The only flower, a crocus furred in grass.
So earth, though black and rich, seemed meaningless
Square wooden houses set in rows
Glared in the teeming sun
And people, feverish, streamed
To newspaper and lawnmower, home
Watched the long twilight come.

London in Retrospect

i

Here holding the mind is the lean rain
Bombarding umbrellas, falling slant upon
Faces unfurled and fresh to the driven sky
Or sheltered by buildings graceful as frozen rain
Shaped to a timely pattern by weathered words—
Fountain songs from a city's mouth.
People surrender to rain, green swayed trees
Bow mutely to the thrashing; dust dovetails
With rivulets between the roots of elms
And weariness is washed from the soul of a square
Dignified by a saint's name, but grown
Grim with the slate grey walls five landings high
Where, discreetly, gas slips through the halls
cathedral chilled, icy with time's rain.

ii

If blackout paint has peeled from pillared doorways
And houses possess new fronts, plain as a starched
Shirt—the occasional lapse, the empty socket
Is no sodden pit, but a pocket of green
Into September paling, into michaelmas purple
Into the golden glint of the sceptre's rod.
For London is royal still, her shabbiness proud
As the poor, her heart pulsing beneath the flesh
An orchestrated underground; her voice
Soaring in Covent Garden, sober on Thames
With song of sails and barges, schooners, smacks:
The men who man them having grown mast-high
To master these times by stars, and not
By the stumbling clocks we're governed by.

Sea Sequence

i

The sea is our season: neither dark nor day,
Autumn nor spring, but this inconstancy
That yet is continent: this self-contained
Organic motion, our mind's ocean
Limitless as thought's range, yet restrained
To narrow beaches, promontories
Accepting her in silence: the land's ear
Forming a concave shell along the sands
To hear sea's shuffle as she leaps in gear
Spuming her poems upon our ribbéd hands
Crying against our poor timidity:
O come to bed in bending water, be
Swept to these arms, this sleep, beloved and proud!
You'll need no linen; nor, thereafter, any shroud.

ii

Now that I walk alone along the stones
I am compelled to cry, like the white gull
Light as snow on the undulating wave
Riding, lamenting. Though he lie
Forever feasting on the sea's blue breast
And I am shorebound, sucked to the hot sand
Crunching the mussels underfoot, scuttling the crabs
And seared by sun—still we are, each one,
The bird, the human, striding a world alone
Calling for colleague who could share the song
Yet bow to the denial: laugh or be mute:
Calling, and yet reluctant to forego
For otherness, the earth's warm silences
Or the loquacious solace of the sea.

iii

I think of you as being continually near
As the sea is, sounding upon the ear
Through night's carousel into dazzling day
In sea's spectacular and changing way.
Sometimes at morning, open-minded, clear
As blue-washed water, never a scowl of foam
Easy to live with, a countenance of home—
Then sudden tempest, lashing out at fear
Moody at folly, clouding out the noon;
Yet through all moods your mind remains the same
Low-breathing or breath-taking, calling the name
Of constancy, whatever time and moon:
With such companion ever at my side
I go alone, not lonely, feeding upon the tide.

The Mirror

Look, old woman,
I know you
I have always known you.
Were these not the parts ever played
—Juliet's nurse
Mad Peer Gynt's mother, Ase
Old servant woman bent upon
A Russian samovar—
The blind woman
By an Irish well?

Now in my fortieth year
I can see my May face
A green nut scarred already
Curling towards a gnarled October.

And the day I was born, surely
I was aged and wrinkled
I came in harassed
Walked on crutches
Slipping on the world.
I grew up rheumatic
Never athletic.
To stoop in garden
Was painful pleasure;
To run on a race day
Exhausted lung power.
Did you not see me at twenty
Stage-struck in bed-ridden parts?

Look for me,
When seventy winters
Have hoarded my hair;
Look for the husk of the years
Falling toward final
Revelation:
My old face a new face growing
Childlike and rounded
Unwrinkled, unbounded
Holidaying
At infinity's station!

LIFE OF THE MIND:
THE 1950S

She makes the words a discipline
The poem a new principle:
From being part singer, dissonant
Now must become the total song.

Vancouver

The city is male, they said: a champion
Caught in a stance; a warrior dreaming.
Indolent he sprawls, arms flung around a mountain
Feet among the Fraser's fishes, head in evergreen.
The city is a sleeper no one dares to waken
Though time is ripe and innocence untaken.

The city is male, they said. Therefore I
Travelled, taking my own pulse.
I was the one who, rigid in Montreal
Froze to steel rails awaiting a frozen tram,
Stalled by a fist of snow on Côte des Neiges.
Steel needled up my spine,
The stiffening hand pointed my time to run.

I was the one who, tensed to northern air
Strode in one dimension through the plains
A dry wind flapping blankets in my face
And as I gasped for air, the dust
Cluttered the ankles, lorried past.
Faster than dust I whirled, I ran.

I, flying in trains
Past sunsets out of Calgary
Felt in each joint the screech and jolt
Of mountains rounded, rivers forded
I swallowed darkness in a tunnel—
Then met, with morning, the huge trees
Like fronded fans in a far valley
Green with the everlasting green
Of coastal rain, of the sea's mutter.

The city is male, they said: smelling the sweat
Squeezed as a log boom's launched
Into False Creek; as a stevedore unloads
The sick-sweet copra; hoists high
The outgoing wheat, matey and muscular.

The city is male and singular
And knows no mate.

The city is male, I said: a hunter haunted
Sniffing the north: on the cool mountain's snow
Seeing a shadow; through the forest floor
Hearing a footfall or an echo go.

Then, with gun cocked—he's taken for a gangster—
Nabbed by his own police, stabbed in the back.
Now bleeding in the dens of Chinatown
Is stuffed in closets, left until the stench
Wrenches the roof off, and explodes the bomb.

O body lying shattered, limbs of man
Tossed in a doorway for the maggot sun:
City unburied, shall I approach you now
Open and undeterred?
What, if your arms say nothing and your mouth
Cries out unheard
Can you awaken yet, out of this sleep
And proclaim the Word?

Bulldozer

The seasick and distracted tree,
Vomiting like madness on disrupted earth
Bellies its branches in one last
Voluptuous sway—and stumbles, smashed.

So in the pit of me some illness rules
Unbalancing my branches: heaving earth,
The vast machine of fear knuckling my roots.
I am tipsy with the reeling times,
The tractor twist of war.

Adam's Choice

We live by prophecy; if anything
Distinguish us as men
(Not beast in field
Nor child in pen)
It is the prophetic dream.

Without your voice
O Baptist, O Mother Shipton
(Freud today, and yesterday Karl Marx)
We should be bent to earth
Aimless as children
In the innocent garden
Secret and hidden.

It was not an apple Eve swallowed
But the Word:
The voice calling forth tomorrow
Became her voice,
And the fear of dying
Without prophesying
Was Adam's choice.

Life of the Mind

Secret she lives, inhabitant
Of silence; of one land;
Yet in the mind
Many times a traveller.

She stands at dawn upon a parapet
Of Sacre Coeur; surveys the blonde, prone
Paris waking up, shutters shooting out
Into the pale washed air; the sweepers picking up
Last night's rose fallen from flowing hair.

Or on a sleepy boat, Thames sauntering,
Surveys from Windsor all the unreal land
Of towers and playing fields,
Trees like stage-props leaning upon heaven—
Is faithful to Big Ben; cathedral calm;
Museums musty out of Aix:
Stone faces smoothed into a patient stance
Amidst the impatient winds
Blistering Marseille; its seaside
Mediterranean only as a name:
Because it bellies up sick grey, afloat
With orange peel and scum, the world's flotsam.

✦ ✦ ✦

Or she is realmed in other consciousness
An age not bloated with conceit
Where there's some innocence
Sleeping out midsummer's heat.

Where children grow in patterns set
And men walk strait-laced to the Lord
Not questioning his powerhouse—
Turbine's engendering the Word.

Community where all men think, yet think alike
Unused to life in an upholstered salon;
Unkempt, uncombed by these fine teeth,
Anxiety's most modern beauty weapon.

✧　✧　✧

Later she is thrust again
Into the early area of pain,
Her own child life; sees children grow
Bruising their branches on the treacherous air;
Not knowing who to strike against, nor where
The evil lurks. Who's enemy? Who's friend?
Who can save you in the end?

Has seen the skipping child strive on
Smiting at the very sun:
From whirling rope and reeling pace
Creating a small universe
Complete—yet wheeling on
Into the new-mown day
The sunny fields of sky.

✧　✧　✧

And has the traveller lost her tongue
Who lives with this abundant throng—
Part of its stream, its melody,
Carried upon—yet strong?

She makes the words a discipline
The poem a new principle:
From being part singer, dissonant
Now must become the total song.

Hop-Scotch

No more the Greek girl dances the cool hours
In dedicated arbour, wreathed with flowers,
Lays violets and amulets upon the stone
And dreams of falling fire and flying bone,
Prays that her secret be made manifest
Only to one, the goddess of her tryst.

Instead she hops upon a pavement, marks
With careful hand the magic stance
Scribbles the mystic names: Ava, Marleen
Throws in her charm and does a one-legged dance.

Pool

The black grass, tarred like negresses
Swarms in the sun
From painted balustrades the children run
And slowly up the spiral stairs
Swimmers vibrate, inhaling air—
Then down, like darts, into precarious blue
Hygienic, chlorinated, true.

The laughter here is free and easy
The shouting at a child-like pitch
The afternoons are long and lazy
And timeless hours lie down and stretch.

But when the night has fallen, Oh
The pool is cold; the lombardies lean over;
An abandoned stage set now,
The concrete gleams, the silence waits.
Look, on the highest diving board
A phosphorescent flash of flesh—
An orator has taken over,
Broods upon the barren water.
The concrete gleams, the silence waits:
As a Greek boy his hand is raised.
Into the listening depths of pool
He hurls his drunken prisons.

Academicals

The Professor as Medium

It depends
Which side you're sitting on
Whether time stands still
Or leaps to merry-go-hand,
Whirls with the giddy clock.

It depends
Whether you sit receptive, with poised pen
Funnelling phrases into hieroglyphs,
Charging the public words
With private hit-and-miss.
The dreamers in this circle weave themselves
Self-mesmerized
Around each number of the clock;
And time is tall,
Its movement imperceptible.

But on the table's other side
He rocks serene:
A medium in contact with the dead.
Their messages
Loom largely in his head,
Their tales are told
Caressingly, the tongue
Fondling the feel of fame.

He pauses for effect: ideas gush,
Intoxicants, out of his storming mouth.
He forms his fountains, geysers, rainbow gales
And sprays them on thin ice
To demonstrate their manufacture,
Soap his sales.

And time for him takes sudden violent bounds:
The clock is crazy and the buzzer mad!
What, bells again? He scowls upon the crowd,
Summons an ectoplasm to withstand the loud,
The emptying door . . .

The Professor and Twins

Professor is shaken:
That one is dumb
Who yesterday
Leaped to the problem
As a dog to a bone:
Gnawed at it,
Pushed it home.

Today he's silent
Sleepy as an owl;
Or as sleek slug on stone
Receives the rain, the sun
And does not turn.

Tomorrow he's alive again!
Revolving doors of days
Perceive him circulating
In and out of class
Now alert, now crass.

Professor suspects some treachery
But holds his peace
Until the pay-off
The last judgment day
When, peering at the rows
Of cropped heads, scratching pens
Perceives not one, but *two*:
A terror and slug
Both poker-faced, and taking notes
And smug!

Professor gasps, and gulps:
Suddenly aghast
Searching now each row
For each one's other ghost.

Professor as Magician

A passionate grammarian, he mounts
The rostrum lightly as a boy
(Although he's old).
The wonder of his toy
Impels him to unfold
His mysteries forthwith—
He drops his handkerchief.

    (And high outside the window, winging-in
    The wintering seagulls pour.
    They mew and mourn
    For summer's crumbs and picknickers—
    Wind-strewn, they sickle, soar.)

"The pattern, gentlemen. Now mark the place!"
He calls his colours and the words fly by
In continents or landmass.
"It is of course a borderline case."
His map arrayed,
The traditional verbs and roots
Must bow and vanish—
Instead he substitutes
His rainbow parish
Of "meaningful word-groups."
With coloured flags his domain is proclaimed,
The marching order of his troops:
Dichotomy!

    (Outside, above the sound
    Of chalk on board
    White-winged birds are flying by
    Flicking the window and the eye—

Uncoloured and unchallenged
The seagulls cry.)

"It is not a matter of either-or"
He waves his wand (a neat cigar).
He does not teach, he conjures up
Or calls, cajoles
The genii from the limbo of the room.
The blackboard swarms—
"Examples of syntactic use"—
The coloured countries fall in form.

He calls! The bird swings, where?
He snatches the white wing
And spreads it wide upon the board:
A wing—a word!

(Outside in sky
The air is peopled by
Terror of seagulls
Ploughing their sea-furrowed
Homeward cry.)

Egg and Square

He calls them dolts and dunderheads:
And yet they are, to all intents and purposes
(As far as one can see)
Human as he:
They have the legs, the arms, the head,
Sleep when they go to bed
Arise at dawn
To hear him spout
Old Xenophon.
And when in spring a leaf
Nudges the uptilled air—
Who would not be
A "square"?

Incognito

She walks as if she might be recognized—
But came on board to be alone.
Out of the corner of her lovely eye
She takes a speedy stock of passengers,

But finds no one. She lights a cigarette
As if a camera recorded her,
As if her thirty years of life had been
A dedication to the screen.

Perhaps you've seen her in a magazine
Swagger in a suntan suit,
Her pale hair scattered to the wind,
Her mouth held mute—

And wondered if she waked or slept,
Ate hamburgers and lived alone?
Observe her now, still walking on "the set"—
Unable to be known.

Loss

I did not hear the trains all night
Nor motor boats in aqueous flight
But loud exploded in my ear
The cardboard cracker box—
Loud with a mouse's fear.

(The trains I did not hear)

The voice I did not hear.
The voice recorded in my sleep
Easy to catch but hard to keep
(O was its message clear?)
I heard my heart beat hail and hammer
The stutter of my tongue's tall stammer

But music from that inmost deep—
The voice I did not hear.

Madrigal

If there is spring—
Burn me.

Summer—
Sigh me green
Wash me in the greenest waves of leaves
Let me be tossed
In streams of sun
And hung
In the cricket's riding-place.

If there is autumn
Turn me round
With the coolest controverted sound
Wind fanning all my fires of leaves,
Winnowing my sheaves.

If winter comes—
Then prop me in the snow
I will be a mute cross of dry wood
Marking the crossroad.

But if there be spring—
Set free, extinguish me with flame.
Harrow me with torches
Blazoning your name.

The Immortals

Those left behind, who grieve
Hang on the living tree like fruit
Unripe for gathering;
Those grieving seem to us
Thieves of the sap, the root.

On earth, all elements
Consistently move out
From darkness into light
From smallness into wholes
And fall away, and fade
Into autumnal blight.

We only, do not grow;
Our centre holds, is still
And folds us multifoliate
Timelessly re-born;
And in this self-completed pause
We neither moan nor mourn.

Surgery

Eye for an eye, tooth for a bleeding tooth
Blood of my blood can saunter through your vein
Distempered by infection or by pain
And be restorative, re-rooted, new.

And soon, the surgeons will predict, our skin
Is interchangable, our kidneys, hearts
All private griefs and self-extending parts:
You make a man of me; I woman you.

Guy Fawkes Night

Lunatic, we watch the fringe of fire,
The leaping shadow dancers hurling bombs
And rockets, whirling catherine wheels,
Laughter exploding in manic moons.

St. George's Square, where the peeled plane trees
Surged at the planet's straining, but withstood
The fire; though the walls crashed inwards, smashed
In rubble of brick and bone, char-blackened wood.

The trees withstood the firey hand of Adam
Who, branding himself, lay in earth's bowels hidden;
Cave man, he huddled beside his shivering kin
To watch his buzz-bombs spit in the eye of heaven.

But the trees survived. New dwellings flank the square.
"A penny for the guy," new Adams cry.
Tonight's rehearsal, flowering the sky
Is for what final act, daring tomorrow's dark?

Walking to Work: London, 1958

The rock and roll of a city is only palpable,
Only real when the city is vast,
Ponderous with human fallout.
Then all the morning bursts its veins.

Out come milkmen with rattling carriers, back and forth
    to the clopping horse;
Out come farm trucks, to roar and swear their way up cleft
    streets behind Covent Garden;
Out come hawkers with barrows to bargain for carrots, filed
    away like sardines, for nestling cabbages, for fluffed heads
    of lettuce, cherub-faced cauliflowers, spears of cucumber;
Out come the demolition crews to tear down the enigmatic
    scroll on the Eighteenth-century doorway;

Out come welders, girded in helmets, to erect the new entrance of
    steel and glass;
Like boys rolling hoops, out come drivers, bouncing empty beer
    barrels from reeking taverns,
Out into the sunlight, onto the trucks.

And by a quarter of nine in the morning
The early scattering of humans scuttling from the Underground
Becomes a slanted stream, steady as rain,
Raindrop faces relishing the sudden sun
Reluctant to dive in
To shop, to office and to whirling wheel—
Reluctant to divide.

And over all the doves flutter and fall
Fall and flutter
And an old man in Trafalgar Square, with long matted hair
Scatters the first crumbs of the morning.
Suddenly from the white tower of St. Martin's bells are shaken
    for their daily airing,
And clang! It is nine o'clock.
On Charing Cross Road
Begins to revolve at the Cameo Theatre
The virgin effigy: Brigitte Bardot
(Restored after last week's rape).
And with a clatter of key-rings, gaolers releasing their prisons,
The iron gates of booksellers, barbers, chemists, collectors,
    jewellers and jockeys
Spring rustily back to the wall.
And the day is unlocked.

Sonnet

These people at the hub, who hold the wheel
See the returning cycle from their still centre,
See the involvement of the spokes, the reel
Of dark and light, crisis and interval.
These pull the parasol; tug at the wheel
Rotating overhead, seek at the stem a face
Holding the whirl; withholding sun or rain
Using the world as shelter, self as base.
These do not blink at sun, encompassing
A whorl of planets spinning at his will:
Dyed in his glow their slow wings open out,
Cry heaven's word; then fold, inviolate still.
If these can spiral in perennial poise—
What angel grapples me? What swan destroys?

Girl

Feeling the poem through my bones
Colouring the bed
An elixir dyeing my dreams
With sinuous red—
By morning, I'm mushroomed
Full blown with the bloom in my head;
Run delicately downstairs
Lest it tremble,
Lest it fall, stone dead.

Letter to My Daughter

We make our own anthologies; pull this blade
Shrieking from its sheath of grass; lay aside
Spiked rosemary in a bottom drawer, until its dust
Rises to steal the air; treasure the dark
Pine-needled wood climbing to sandy caves
Fragments of history in a broken vase—
Who set the terra cotta beaches in their place
Marked out by rhythmic hands? Is this
A circle in the sand where fire once flamed?
A woman knelt? The rocking, shaking world,
Green earthquakes, tidal wave of blood
Bursting the dam, wrenching wide the womb
Until the mother's scream is silenced by
Strange note, extraordinary feat: the newborn wail.

So you, unarmoured one, through corridors of blood
And walls of bone, your fleet feet echoing.
Lightness was there, a kind of airiness
But toughness at the bone; as grass resists being pulled
So you clung to the mother place
The first wild garden where a cherry tree
Blazed its white bliss upon your second year
And bled for you each birthday.

Uprooted from that place, harried by war
The blare of radio, the deadly tramp of feet
Narrowed to walk upon a surly street
And stamp the pavement white with August heat
And stumble up the wooden steps to show
A red rose clenched, wrenched from a neighbour's wall
(A rose the first love ever felt, the living scent
Something outside yourself, and separate)
But screamed to feel the thorn that pierced; and shaken
By sight of blood; by accidents
And ships being bombed and sunk
The buzz bombs hissing from the tender sky:
All the green world distorted, on its back
Roots clawing upward, seared by pitiless sun.

—You held this in your being, and became
An undine shrivelling in the blast,
Strange laughter shaking you with fits at night,
Words in your head a fiery bottleneck
Corked tight for lack of language;
Hearing our speech, knowing the sound and tone
Of meaning, but too innocent to seize
The mother tongue and make it all your own.

When you began to talk, the world turned over:
The armies vanished into words, the men
Returned to fathering. And once again
Lights flashed upon the hill;
The leaning cherry tapped your window-pane
Washed its green hands in the September rain.

Ten years after, how you tilt the world
Your own way; hold out arms for love,
Believe, believe, the impossible golden fruit
Will shower down; and that the tree will speak;
Interpreter of all your silences.
So, tip toe as a dancer before music's start,
I see you eager to begin; and dance you must
Although new rhythms weave you unaware
From sunshine into shade; from blue air down to dust.
But dance you will; become a tree you will
Rooted within your heritage, but throwing wide
Your leaves by wind's will freed; and offering love
Not in the mind, but in the very proof—
The dancer and the dance identified.

Fasten Safety Belts

The gnarled, the wrinked and the white-notched sea
Is framed below my leaning eye
And on the wide verandah-wing of plane
NO STEP, the words are written red.

It is well said:
There is no step
From haven into heaven.
Below, last night, a ship
Cracked in the ice
Men spilled in foam:
The gnarled, the wrinkled and the white-notched sea
Is sepulchre, is home.

And on this funnelled aileron,
The helmeted, projecting one
(God's gondola)
A circled eye, exhaust pipe, gives
A God's eye view!
Sees, walking on tumbled water
A figure framed, that flows
Into infinity;
And as his halo gold horizon
Changes, to blaze magenta, rose.

What matter if grey matter
Has no scheme?
Dawn severs the dull skull,
I cogitate, *I* dream!

Words for Our Time

i

Early or late
day is descending
losing light

This morning room
warm tiles in sleepy sun
this will be taken soon
the chairs and tables stripped and dumb

And time today is doom
washing away, swept under
never by pygmies used for building towns
never an air-spun ladder.

ii

We live with night, and its
unscented and impersonal sky
gardened with fiery blooms
indifferent where they die

We seek destruction, dark
lit only by incendiaries
our air must be
choked with blazing fires.

Lately, our children grow
in burrows, limp to life
with splintered bones, dulled ears
barren, fear-filled eyes.

Our day is mockery:
defenders, all, we rout
its fiercest penetration, and
let shrink the noonday heart.

Siesta creeps on limbs
too weak for love or hate:
man's upright mind is down
thinking disintegrates.

iii

Now, early or late
who is there left to say
one word for charity
for an arousing day?

Who is there left to see
wood's rim through rosy fingers
blue shadows lift
from muddy edge of rivers?

Who now can drink
the brimming cup of morning
challenge the taut, black sky
with our death's warning?

In the Ward

i

The boy in the next room
Is busy on bones.
"The surgery exam," he says
"I zipped through in no time flat—
But O the curse
Of gynecology!"
He wants to be come a medical practictioner
In Alberta
(Where medicine isn't free—
Thinks he.)

ii

The girl beyond
Is the one I imagined myself to be.
When she thinks no one's looking
She twists herself into the shape of a tree.
As we pass up and down the stairs
Starting a breeze
Her leaves dance
Obliquely.

iii

At the top lair
Old woman by window
Is counting, counting
What buyers pass
And pass her by
What hours creak
Whistle and cry
Till darkness climbs the stair.

iv

Around the corner
(Pale monk in a black cell)
The polio child
Lies in his iron bell
Saying, with furtive fingers,
The beads of his hell.

v

At midnight Big Ben
Booms.
"Old time?" I stumble from sleep,
"Has the time changed?"
"Yes, and times have changed too, I expect"
Says the ghost at my elbow—
The old gentleman who died in this room.

vi

So I
Thieving in and out
Of these
I too am ghost and breeze—
Clothe myself
In their rags and tears.

Côte d'Azur

Seized by sun, its blows
Striking through flesh to bone,
Crevassing ribs to reach
The palpable stone

We lie deep in the dazed
Remembrance of time past
Our ancient chain of sun
Never unclasped

Our eyes never withdrawn
From Africas beyond
Magnified, through glass
Setting afire the sand—

How sudden now, to wake
Caught in a chill wave,
The raw air mourning us
The afternoon gone grave:

Through the tossed mane of seas
Horizon draws a comb:
Sun falls upon its knees
The numb north pulls us home.

Invocation

Descend   descend
angel to whom I turn
spirit for whom I burn
at windows where the chestnut trees
burnish the sky
in parks where fountains play
wind-twisted chords on cool
indifferent stone—
descend   atone
for all your absences
and my intransigence.

I have been
peopled with faces
haunted   grim
in my dream
no blazed wing
upheld my fantasies:
they fell like curling chestnut leaves
paper thin to the tongues of wind.

I have been
absent from facility awhile:
bear with my brutish
burrowings in earth
my unattending ear:
lean, loving, and attest:
widened   these doors
will honour the intricate light
bow to the blazen guest.

Spring in Russell Square

People in deck chairs are spattered
Splashing the paths like geraniums
Lolling and spilling over
Onto forbidden greenness.

Trees toss at their moorings
Outrageously planting new flags
In empire of blue air
A blackbird on lookout duty
Cries heave-ho
To pigeons popping below
Chattering tulip faces
Clasp hands and bow.

About the monument of Bedford
Smiling in bold bronze
Office girls curl with cupids
Whirl parasol skirts
Toss sandwiches, munch words.
And the young men sauntering, eyeing
New-fashioned flounces of tulip
Are dusk-red roamers, wallflowers
Appraising the fluttering females.

You can't have a bench to yourself
Not these days, can you?
Reproves the well-scrubbed old woman
Squeezing herself and her blind husband
Beside the young lovers.

And they stop whispering
Speak hand to hand only
Toe writing in the gravel.
Be my love, his body is saying
Kneel
And let me feel
Your foolhardy hair
Striking to windward.

Hold still. Hold still.
I feel you flowing
In my breasts, she is replying
Shifting her eyes from sun
Suddenly blinded.

But the old man and the old woman
Sit separate, silent
Sigh
As a bird wing flashes
On the pool of remembrance.

And beyond the hemmed green hemisphere
And dove-tailed park
The traffic's tempest
Roars round the clock.

Man on Grouse Mountain

Last skier swung on the last lift
Is swirled away in the sucking drift
Down the sheer mountain into valley's night
Where fir trees ache with cold and cedar trees
Turn into birds, web-winged, snowwhite.

The watcher at the wheel lets the last man go on,
Wires whirring overhead (and churning slow) as chair swings down
Listens to catch the words flung against sky
Till snowwhirl muffles even that goodbye:
Snow bats about his face like moths at night
And darkness pitches forward toward his light.

The watcher turns the motor off; and with a bang
The chains skip, swing; the wires clang;
And light goes out. Only his lantern now
Forces him down the gangway like a plough
Cutting the snow, breaking the ice to guide
The last man moving on the mountainside.

Once within, the door bangs at his blow
He stamps he feet, scattering clods of snow
Feels fumbling the electric switch; and is alone
In the great timbered hall, on hearth of stone
Stirring the logs to make a faster flame.
And is alone; a man without a name.

Miles below, if he could see
Through storm's white butterflies
Beyond the country of the trees
(Steady at the root and heart)
Beyond the river's foaming start
The Capilano's curling plume
Across the spillway and the boom
Come signals of hot pulsing light
Probing the network of the night;
Lurches with a sickening roar
The man-made shore.

He did not make it, so he will not seek it:
Did not lift his hand to harm a lamb
Nor push a neighbour forward
Did not dig a stint to build a dam
Nor electrify a railroad
Did not approve
And so could never love
Fellers of forest, builders of better homes,
Television towering
Or all the organized invention
Preventing natural selection.

He will have none of it. Having lost the hope
Of solace or support, he turns away
Pushes the logs together, stronger
(Something to tend within his scope).
Wrestling with men left him his old hunger:
He'll wrestle with a mountain, now
It will last him longer.

Last skier swung on the last lift
Is swirled away in the sucking drift
Down the sheer mountain into valley's night
Where fir trees ache with cold and cedar trees
Turn into birds, web-winged, snowwhite.

Paysage Provençale

i

Cézanne recorded it forever, yet
His memory and mine are juxtaposed.
He saw the shouting green of pines, drinking the sun
(I see the juniper clinging to the rock)
He saw the summer season casting cypresses
Like knives against a yellow ochre wall
(I see the owl dusting the dusky tree)
He played his line for shafts of darting gold
To knot with ribboned olive trees. He linked tile roofs
With bleeding orange earth; tethered the plane trees
To his brush; set Ste. Victoire afloat,
A long stone gull soaring to the north.
(I see how clouds subdue his burnished blaze,
Silver his landscape with December's breath.)

ii

In winter, along the chateau's avenues
Of fallen plane-tree leaves the mottled trees
Seem bound in stone by immemorial arms:
Frozen images of man and woman
Woven together and yet separate,
Treading the park where voiceless fountains play
Out of the mouths of frogs, immured alive—
Treading the avenues eternally.
And by the orchard garden, lost in thought,
A dreaming Venus hewn of roughened stone
Gazes, as if she saw Antiquity,
Beyond the wars of Saracen and Saint,
Beyond the rattle of the chariots
Ploughing red loam, scanning the sky for gods.

iii

Breathless, I turned to climb the hill for moss,
For Christmas holly and sweet rosemary;
Stood on that stoney ridge, level with clouds
That rippled pink on purple, fold on mauve fold
As the old sun lowered his gold beard
Into the silent pines; and stopped by me.
What creatures then out of the templed wood
Were winged above me on the vibrant air
And swept me down the hillside to a cranny where
Moss grew the greenest, holly shone with fire.
Rooted within that glade I saw time past
Gliding a rocket into things to be—
But man like moss, still clinging to the ground.
Cézanne, these secret fountains have I found.

The Gift

The painting livens
                      livens me lives ay
Plants phalanxes of dark
                          forbidding stone
Around a tree quite plain
                         plane tree *platane*
Green in glory of May
Lets sunlight sink its shaft
Into a well of wall
                   all well
And ochre
           ochre light
                  takes over.

Now I am peering down
                   down
To unseen passers-by
Paris by day, by spring
                     handspringing on
And I on tightrope of suspense
Suspend the green
                exuberance
And in a dazing somersault
                  dance.

Sunflowers

The French *aperitif*
is rightly named
for it doesn't send to sleep
(as rum, saki, tequila)
but stings awake.

Swaying on a stem
I burst
into the sun's mouth.

COLOUR OF YOUR TALKING:
THE 1960s

The colour of your talking
is a strange adventure
I am dyed in the warp
and woof of its structure

Self-Portrait

And from your mouth, my own misshapen teeth.
My mother's eyes; in mine no cornflowers grew,
Leaves raced, the summer danced.
Your fine hair, father, scattered all too thin—
No silver wires curling in the wind
Like hers, I'll have. His pointed chin,
Her jaw, plain cussed, stubborn to the point
Of senselessness; at other times sheer pluck,
A gay insouciance sprang from the set of it.

Her narrow hand, fine, and yet all thumbs,
Object of his mockery, I share; a hand
Good for picking roses; guiding a pen.
The awkward girl-legs running in the wind
She must have had; their complement,
The rounding shoulders hunched above a book.
He hated it. "Stand up straight for God's sake, girl!
Chin in!" (Destroying the pleasure of a walk
Sowing the self-distrust.) Her beauty such
No child could rival it, and yet I sensed
Her hatred of the body's good, not understood
Until one morning naked in a wood
I flew to find the joy in it.
I hugged a trembling birch, white-skinned
And found it kin; I lay long in the sun
Ever becoming one with crushed leaf-mould.
The green spears pricking through
Tingled my flesh, the wrinkles of the earth
Pressed patterns on my skin and bone
No years erase; till fossil I become.

Benny Lighting a Fire

He knows the wood.
Each piece he judges instantly
places it right: below, beside, above.
He knows the wood, as if it sprang
out of his loins, extension of his hands.
"Paper"? I ask.
(There must be added element
inflammable.)
He smiles, inscrutable.
Only a match is struck.
As wood explodes, he leans beside—
his body crackling, chuckling.

The Child on Steps

The child on steps playing "jacks"
with a small rubber ball
bouncing into hand gone sore
from scraping the paint and the wood's cracks
snatching at metal knuckle bones —
the barren dice—
the child on an evening in April
facing alone the fall of day
while across the street laughter is ringing
boys wrestling, girls taunted and teased
flashing their new-won sex
their rounded legs and sudden swollen breasts—
the child feeling and knowing
but not belonging
is no more lost than I, now in this evening weather
sundowner on an African verandah
tossing the words, tossing the words far
and catching emptiness.

Fire

Only the gnarled
Root of a tree
Suits my appetite
Curls my tongue
I whirl and whorl
Lick hungrily
The deep coiled snarl
Of the old shoot

Like a tooth
Grown longer in the grave
The word protrudes
Its blunt old root
Into my gaping snout.

The Still Centre

We come back to the poem:
music vanishes
sound vibrates, fades
but the words of our poem
can be tried on, over and over—
the words fit
like silence in a room
clothing it, filling the corners
hovering above

O my love
your voice vanishes as you turn a corner
your figure weaving through trees, becomes a tree
but the words left lying in my hands
the poem fluttering
speaks, and sings in my hand
over and over

speaks and sings

Living Room

My room is a small grove
of hemlock, oak
on each side packed with moss
rock bouldered

gold green with moss the rock glows
I lean there, on the rock's right hand
for morning sunlight

early, I bathe
I come out of icy water
a cool white stream of skin
curled over pine cones

in the sun
my breasts are round cold stones
flowing
       flowing

in the late hours
I move, back to a pine tree, back to the lake,
and look uphill past four hemlock
locked to arbutus death-in-life
(for the dead leaves cling
to the new green)
their red boils glisten, split
and the green under bark shines like raw skin

at evening I reverse myself
crouched back to rock
facing the lake
the long shadows—
the gong of sun
going going
sets pools on fire
water accepts the blaze
reaches to take
the sky's last messages.

Cockcrow

At the periphery and fringe
of villages where drumming swings
I hear the summons   leap from bed
and dance from darkness
into the sun's round red

The hand that does the drumming
moves the world
meets sun halfway
and hauls him over the rim
sets wings in iridescence
into a tail spin

The hand that does the drumming
drums man home
to womb and woman
beats that rhythm
on black curving thighs
thrusts love upward

Africa

From the twentieth of November
At the turn of the moon's tide
I entered the dark continent:
It was blazing with light.
In Nairobi the streets glittered like yellow glass
The buildings were pure columns of white;
Trees tossing on the skyline were a pale violet
(The jacarandas)
Trees in the parkway were firelit
(Flaming flamboyants)
Black men sauntering the streets
Clothed in white
Lifted their faces, polished, to the sun.
Wind rippled the fountains.

From the twentieth of November
I entered the resplendent sunlight
Deceptive as gold.

The colour of your talking . . .

The colour of your talking
is a strange adventure
I am dyed in the warp
and woof of its structure

you roll out panoramas
carpets of flowers
the eye lost in distance
becomes ear, listening

or else you are peremptory
and the colours sharpen
to microcosmic green—
the tree trembles

or else your voice is darkness
under and above me
I fall into black branches
whirl on a dark axis.

View North

I feel this land moored to a northern pole
reeling and straining
jockeying on oceans

I hear, locked in night's hold
the subterranean rock creaking and groaning
the thrust of barnacles
knocking on gunwales
shrill crescendo of gulls
slapping the water
laughter of dolphins

I see
sea's turbulent darkness
prowl on the pronged floor
probing the pattern

In storm
hard against icebergs the shore lunges
and we are with it
we are pulled north, circled by iccfloes
and sun at dead midnight
rips the door from its hinges.

It's Time

It's gone. The frontier's gone
and shunting rivers have shifted your mountains, Walt
to a pile of rubble.
It's time to move your barbaric yawp
rolling over alfalfa westward:
but the prairie's gone
oil bubbles from its blackened throat
"first crocuses!" no children cry
no croak of crows
machine-made cranes
rip at the sky.

> The frontier's gone, Walt
> we haven't the eyes for frontiers anymore:
> through our contact lenses
> we can scarcely make out
> the golden circuit of the hand
> or what it's for.

It's time to go, Walt
down to the western sea
where fish float dead and bloated
on bleary water
where the excreta of millions
fouls the whale's home.

> It's time to call a halt
> and start again your warning
> before they tie up world's bundle
> set it afire
> and send it hurling outward
> to smash another star.

Completion

No need to speak
we do not need to say
the everyday remark:
other marks are made

No need to gesture
or defend
a vehement spark
we touch as friend to friend

No need to question:
when we put out the light
these worlds unfolding
pile dark on tremulous dark

The light is out
no need to read
who read
by bodies' light

Unable as I am . . .

Unable as I am
to throw away old letters
    (yet I do not read them)
or erase old tapes
    (yet I do not hear them)
unable to discard
    echoes   echoes
    reverberating senselessly
taking up rooms
    I should sweep clean
Unable to plunge clear
    over the border
It's no wonder I
walk so encumbered:
love runs rings around me
I fatten as the oak
on last year's growing.

Widow

My wedding ring was not of gold
but steel, gold-covered
and grown close to bone
to be sawed off.

Death cut it, finally.

Free in the sun
the bent finger straightens.

Sky Watchers

Those shaken shepherds leaning on the night
I like to think were Okanagan men
seated around their campfire by the Lake
mourning with drums the loss of a young girl
taken with fever—borne sudden away
beyond the scent of sagebrush underfoot,
beyond the sight of sunflower-slanted grass.
The drums accelerate. The ritual masks,
the feathered figures circle in the dance.
And suddenly a chief looks up, old woman cries:
for heaven has opened! Sky's roof tilted down
pours a green radiance over hills;
lake water crackles with an orange flame.
The silence stuns. A young man, stumbling, drums
alone; stands up alone, moves in a drugged daze
lifts voice to find the high, shrill notes
the jewelled and the studded words . . .
Aurora borealis, later men will name
reduce by name and make most reasonable
the fire's unreason—madness in the eye,
the human figure hammered to the sky.

Statues

Eurydice

Between us words must fly
on music's page
tempered, from love's cry
to an articulate rage.

To love you without speech
is to be free for faring:
subtle as a beast
and salmon-daring.

Yet how I long to shout
my loving, from the lungs:
turn the head about
and speak with tongues!

Persephone

Not he, the naked sun,
bids me wear widow's weeds
nor she, whose silver nudity
waxes and wanes, yet ever grows undressed:
eternal elements require no ornament
beat, in their single fixity
behind the pounding heart
or shine as phosphorous within the bone:
our body dresses them.
But trembling things, the trees,
Demeter's kingdom; green and mauve
anemones
these I resemble.
I, like these,
fear the down-going
wear my grief in leaves.

The Elms

When I was young
the trees grew free and easy
greening against
the summer sky

I lived against elms
—Can't you remember?
teens, leaning out
of a bedroom window
Toronto, the Twenties—

and elms in autumn
stripped
trunks interlacing
loving
their branches against evening sky
a brilliant hieroglyph
veins moving
soaked in India ink
startling!

    Tell me tell me tell me elm
    tell me tales of Shaun or Shem

    On ne sait jamais
    la puissance des arbres

Now I sit again at a bedroom window
maritime, autumnal
and the elms surprise me
I greet them as sisters:
this tree
struck long ago
its roots in me
and the web of its movement
against sky woven
is the web of my life:

intricate   corroded
but somehow proven.

The Hammer and the Shield
(A Found Poem)

Tomorrow we shall meet
Death and I—.
And he will thrust his sword
Into one who is wide awake.
     —Dag Hammarskjöld, "Thus It Was"

The unicorn is not abnormal
Because it has no mate.
     —Elizabeth Brewster, "Dag Hammarskjöld: Near Martyr"

i

Take a log
    Nyerere said
between two men:
a log hewn out
    makes a canoe
it travels distances
    and can be used
for fishing

But take a log
    and haul it by yourself
it's almost
    useless.

Two men must plan to go
    the same way
        in the same canoe
to win a fish and build a camp
two men must go
    together.

This was the lesson taught
    by Dag Hammarskjöld
—commented the lean African
    Nyerere.

ii

From Vasa Castle, Upsala
into battle your forebears went
defending the land
with hammer and with shield

But your later ancestors
consolidated, compromised
became administrators, statesmen—
your father a Prime Minister
of Sweden.

It was not expected
that at nineteen, in the listener's gallery
you heard words resounding
            from the deep past
into your conscience:

> *Who takes the initiative*
> *who exerts influence*
> *is so utterly immaterial*
> *compared to the one great question:*
> *to make our country*
> *secure for the future.*

But for Sweden, early
the boundaries extend early
(thinking of the world)
and your father also taught you:

> *Being neutral*
> *is not a question of saying yes*
> *to both sides*
> *but of saying no.*

Thus you learned to say "no" publicly
to both sides
but in private, you found
a need for "yes."

I don't know Who—or what—put the question.
I don't know when it was put.
I don't even remember
     answering.

But at some moment I did answer Yes to Someone—
     or Something—
and from that hour I was certain that existence
     is meaningful
and that, therefore, my life, in self-surrender,
     had a goal.

From that moment I have known what it means
     "not to look back,"
and "to take no thought
     for the morrow."

iii

What would a man be
who had the mark
of so much good on him?
How would he breathe and be?

          Is my contact with others
          a contact of reflections?
          Who or what
          can give me the power
          to transform a mirror
          into a doorway?

Your friend, Auden, the poet
explained you, this way:
"An exceptionally aggressive
     super-ego"
the tie with his father?
A Hammarskjöld shall do better
               shall be better
than other men.

"On the other hand,
an ego weakened
by a 'thorn in the flesh' ":

    (for himself he could see
    no joy in loving
    no lifelong marriage)

To be
or not to be?
That was the question.
He was fascinated
by his own problem.

        Because it never found a mate,
        Men called
        The unicorn abnormal.

        ✧   ✧   ✧

        What makes loneliness an anguish
        Is not that I have no one to share my burden,
        But this:
        I have only my own burden to bear.

iv

Such you were
when the world found you:
August, 1953
you assumed the mantle
"the most impossible job
in the world"
Secretary-General
of the United Nations.

        In our era,
        the road to holiness
        necessarily passes through
        the world of action.

You acted:

In Peking, 1955
your diplomacy
freed the American airmen

At Suez, 1956
your action, rejecting
the ultimatum
of France and Britain,
affirmed:

> *The principles of the Charter*
> *are, by far, greater*
> *than the Organization*
> *in which they are embodied....*

> *The Secretary-General ...*
> *must also be the servant of the Charter,*
> *and its aims must ultimately determine*
> *what for him is right or wrong.*
> *For that he must stand.*

Out of Suez
Sunday, November 4
A United Nations Force
came into being:
Canada's suggestion,
your initative.
And you acted, further
In Hungary, Lebanon
Jordan and Laos
until the moment
of the dark encounter:
Congo.

June, 1960
the Belgians gave
the Congo its independence:
but they did not let go.
The new Premier, Patrice
Lumumba,
struck the warning:
"We wish to be free
from the ironies, the insults
the blows we have had to submit to
morning noon and night—
because we are black men."
He demanded action
    from the United Nations:
an army to oust the Belgians
an army to quell Katanga
where Moïse Tschombé
refused to be part
of the new nation.

    "A crisis of war or peace!"
    you told the Security Council.
    Even if the Belgian troops
    were staying on "to maintain order"
    presence was unacceptable
    to the peoples of the world.

I strongly recommend to the Security Council
that it authorize the Secretary-General
to take the necessary steps,
in consultation with the Government of the Congo,
to provide the Government with military assistance.

You were given
a free hand:
Belgian troops must withdraw.
4000 African troops
        from Ghana, Ethiopia
                Morocco, Tunisia
were on their way.
But you insisted on neutrality:

> This U.N. Force *could not be party*
> *to any internal conflict;*
> *it could not take the initiative*
> *in the use of armed force,*
> *but is entitled to respond with force*
> *to an attack with arms.*

Your gesture was generous:
but it was not
sufficient.
Against the new nationalism
and cries of "oust the Belgians"
"quell Katanga"
you counselled:

> *Do not expect from us actions*
> *which might jeopardize the future happiness*
> *of those we wish to help.*

But Lumumba, fiery
a nationalist whose magnetism
rallied the Congo
cried out in protest:
"The battle must be to the strong!"
"Why are your blue berets
        your Swedish bodyguard
so helpless? Why don't they help us
to fight?"

> *These are not soldiers of war;*
> *but soldiers of peace.*

147

Your words were not understood.
In the midst of "neutrality"
you were cornered in a three-way
triangle:
by the Belgians, supporting Katanga
as a separate country led by Tschombé;
by the Americans, supporting Kasavubu
and his Congolese army;
by the Russians, supporting
Patrice Lumumba, patriot
beloved of the people.

And Moscow cried out,
Kruschev accused you:
"While there are neutral countries
there are no neutral men!"
A journalist reported:
"It is now the view of the Soviet Government
that there is no such thing
as an impartial civil servant."

> *To be*
> *or not to be.*
> *Ambiguous word, "neutrality."*
> *I have come to see its pitfalls . . .*
> *We have to deal here with a question*
> *of integrity . . .*
> *a question of conscience . . .*

*If the international civil servant knows himself to be
free from such personal influences in his actions and
guided solely by the common aims and rules laid down
for and by the Organization he serves and by recog-
nized legal principles, then he has done his duty, and
then he can face the criticism which, even so, will be
unavoidable. . . . If integrity in the sense of respect for
law and respect for truth were to drive him into posi-
tions of conflict with this or that interest, then that
conflict is a sign of his neutrality . . . it is in line with
his duties as an international civil servant.*

Brave words—but cold.
For often the truth
is cold
snow cold.
Against it the flames
leaped
fire devoured the country—
Katanga against Congo—
Tschombé against Kasavubu—
Lumumba caught, in between
held captive suddenly
in his residence
by the Congolese National Army.

    The U.N. forces
    stood by, on duty
    but on orders
    of the Secretary-General
    could not take action
    or interfere
    when, in the dead of night,
    a car swept into the compound:
    it carried Lumumba northwards.

    It was not long
    before he was captured:
    on December 2, 1960,
    at Port Francqui—
    brought by armed Congolese
    to Leopoldville.
    An eyewitness
    from the United Nations
    recorded it: saw him

        "without his glasses
          soiled shirt
            hair in disorder
              blood on his cheek
              hands tied
                behind him"

December 2.

The tension increased.
In the noonday heat
Their wills began to waver.

Night flared
Phosphorescent,
The jungle wailed in the fierce grip of the storm.

They paid
The full price of love
That others might enjoy a victory.

Morning mist
Chirping of early birds.
Who recalled the night's sacrifice?

On December 3, from your U.N. mountain
you heard that Lumumba
had been taken to Camp Hardy
where he was held
under "inhuman conditions
of health and hygiene."
You called Kasavubu
to desist, in the name of
the Universal Charter
of Human Rights—
without avail.

December 3.

The road,
You shall follow it.

The fun,
You shall forget it.

The cup,
You shall empty it.

The pain,
You shall conceal it.

The truth,
You shall be told it.

The end,
You shall endure it.

Two months later
on February 3, 1961
Moïse Tschombé announced:
"Patrice Lumumba
was killed trying to escape"
by villagers near his gaol.
At the U.N. headquarters
the Soviet Union withdrew its recognition
of Dag Hammarskjöld
as Secretary-General.
All over the world
the clamor was carried:
your name was sullied.

Tired
And lonely,
So tired
The heart aches.
Meltwater trickles
Down the rocks,
The fingers are numb,
The knees tremble.
It is now,
Now that you must not give in.

On the path of the others
Are resting places,
Places in the sun
Where they can meet.
But this
Is your path,
And it is now,
Now that you must not fail.

Weep
If you can,
Weep,
But do not complain.
The way chose you—
And you must be thankful.

So you tried again:
this time, to bring back Katanga
into a United Congo
to meet with Tschombé
persuade him to call a cease-fire
to end the attacks on U.N. detachments
to end the firing on U.N. planes.

I suggest that I should meet you
personally,
so that we can together try
to find peaceful methods
of resolving the present conflict,
thus opening the way
to a solution of the Katanga problems
within the framework of the Congo.

I am awaiting
your urgent reply.

It was Tschombé who received the message
was notified
of the rendezvous.
It was Tschombé who
did not reply.
But you set out anyway
from the Northern Congo
in a DC 6 B—Swedish Transair:
September 17, 1961.

We were listening
on the Copperbelt
at the end of the dry season
the time when, in the parklands
acres of trees around Ndola
hugged their silence
their dust-choked dryness.

Near midnight, above
in the vast pocket of sky
pinpricked with myriad
               silver
a speck circled
a humming was centred
               recorded
Was it Dag Hammarskjöld
coming in for a landing?
The control tower was listening
alerted
and we heard of it
at midnight
on the Copperbelt radio:
he'd be coming in
he'd do the job.
But half an hour later
he had not landed.
"Plane not heard from."
Startled, we sat up, tense
rubbed the sleep from our eyelids—
for an hour, waiting.

No news.
We slept then, uneasy
and at 7 a.m.
turned on the radio.
There had been a flash, sighted
at midnight
over Mufulira:
then the fatal
silence.

Waking,
Now fully awake,
I heard the scream
That had woken me up.

✧ ✧ ✧

Far away,
For the last time
I heard the scream,
The scream of terror
The voice of loneliness
Screaming for love.

Who the quarry,
Who the silent hunter
Over the sea of mist
Among the black trees,
Long before dawn?

Remembered other dreams
Of the same mountain country:
Twice I stood on its summits,
I stayed by its remotest lake,
And followed the river
Towards its source.
The seasons have changed
And the light
And the weather
And the hour.

But it is the same land.
And I begin to know the map
And to get my bearings.

Côte d'Azur

i

What skin is this? A superimposed encasement
rubber-enforced, congealed
like plastic glass, over the body's stance
a prison of transparencies
light-stroked, water-woven
a garment fit to travel into
regions of darkest water.

Jacques put it on, and dived.
I felt him far below
surveying weeds, assessing rock
seizing on blue-tailed fish he had not known before,
revelling in coral.

ii

The Mediterranean has no tides,
is not moon-grounded; her blue limpid
inactivity
is static in itself
though winds whip up white storms, rains lash
her shores, her harbours, foreshore fortified
and flood the towns; pour through the brick-built sluices
ruin for villages; demolish restaurants
with their umbrella'd esplanades, waiters alert
with napkins and raised tray; defy the menu
soupe du jour; romp with white teeth and curling tongues.

iii

We drove out, Jacques, the engineer, and I
to survey the last damage. The storm's backlash
still lacerated fishing-shacks, tore up the conduits
of the villages.
Along the sandy shore
the waves still roared
licking their chops;
I listened to the sound
and heard no language; only tongues of doom
panting for conquest.

Jacques, examining
the damage to the seabreaks and the conduits
spat out his quarrel:
the Mediterranean has no tides
but has her temperaments:
is vicious yet—
threatens our sunlit life
our crystal diving.

Fundy
(For L. A. D.)

How far will the tide come
pressing its power
against my banks
meeting my waters in a swirling foam
of probe and pressure
eddy and release?

My body stretches long,
reptilic
dark on the brightest day
and somnolent
until, each tide
I open wide my limbs
the curling tidal tongues
leap into me and turn
my river into ocean.
Into my crevices

crabs crawl
the lobster mailed in dark green shell
the slithery salmon silver in its leap
small smelts, the bumbling halibut
elusive clams—
all living swimming things
pour into me!
Become a whale,
I pant upon the shore
shout with a whale's roar.

And then I yield
my wracked and earth-wrenched roots
my granite beach
through raging rocks I pour
my waters back
until again your plunging body pounds
my farthest shore.

Under that blazed sea-sky
the shimmering sands, long-limbed
reveal the rhythm of the waves
and sun sheds light
upon the river bed's dark name.

At Birney's
(June 4, 1967—before the Israeli-Arab conflict)

Sitting there on the floor
in the sleek easiness
of eating and drinking
of listening to poets—so young—
reading aloud
their private commitments

We sensed the rivalries
        entanglements
but believed nonetheless and said so
that the world was essentially
round and solid
brimming over with good things:
it could not run over
into sour war.

Jostling politely
to hear ourselves repeated
on the tape recorder
we kept on thinking
that tomorrow would be Monday
and not June 5.

We thought we were living and growing.
Now, in the mirror
we notice the withered eyes
the unerasable frown.
Now, by due process of hate
we have begun
to die.

Aliens All

We are not at home, here,
In dreams are swept to far shores
where men work to build in sand
a temporary castle
or in underground caves
        amid stalactites and stalagmites
struggle to create crystal
and have no care that it is ice, not glass
and falls apart at the least tremble.
In that blue, sun-glittering country
we fly with snow
alight on verdant valleys
and on the day after
fashion incredible sculptures
recreating ourselves
snow men, snow women
or neuter children

We are not at home here, knowing
how it might be, in a land flowing with milk and honey
where we are divers, drowning and resuscitating
where the winds caress the teats
        so they give forth milk
where bees sting the tongue
and words become honey.

We are not at home here
being haunted by
        other music—
green of another country.

The Feedback

Sudden eruption of green
against my window
(elm leaves affirming)
blots out the tiers
of apartment concrete.
Town almost becomes
      country.
But there's no blotting out
for the ears, traffic-soaked;
there's no antidote to sirens.
The nagging moan of motors
on Spadina speedway
fills every crack
of silence.
        I must re-teach my ear
        to hear only the sparrow's shouting.

Persephone

Time tells me I am not
so tall as I once was
and not so small
grown closer to the ground
and spreading round
I feel affinities
with cabbages
turnips and beets
all firm things
that hold their roundness
close
to earth or under it
tasting the brown feel
of the turned-up autumn soil
breathing the undercold.

POEMSNAPS
(Vancouver)

Acorn

In the black cavern
of the jazz den
they've conjured you up
under red lights:
You: husky torso
brawny arms
bawdy mouth
you toss your head
   (prize fighting)
delve down
shovel another poem in place
   and
     SHOUT IT!

      Bissett

    Any man's
    Bill or Jack
    he demands
    beans talk
    says writing a poem
    is just throwing a rope
           high
         sky
    and climbing up on it
    hand
      over
        hand

Mayne

Seymour
hangs out his trousers
on anybody's clothesline
(for all the neighbours to see)

The devil take the hindmost—
says he

Lane

"Savage mind"
yet body so
gentle
seeking always
softness in women
      but awaking   cold
      a beaten beach
      the strewn gulls   crying

Lowther

Standing on the wide   sun-dazzled
stone steps
a courthouse   love-in
we hear your lullaby
for a napalm baby
we see you suddenly
frail   piercing   yet surrounded
daughter of
ten thousand Grecian women

Between a Thousand

Sometimes
        on the television
there's this   flickering and fogging
faces   out of focus
places   no place
and the snow

        the eternal television snow
           falling

It isn't unusual   however
living is like this   also
between a thousand photographs of you
           juxtaposed
flashed in a second

I have to choose   whom I love
          who you are

A Threnody: Easter, 1968
(for Martin Luther King)

Here we wait, under the fresh-brimmed sun
in the deep of the pine wood
last year's needles brown and bruised
last year's snow   a white shadow
      hugging the hollows
and the river below
flowing again in patches
sloshing its ice chunks
into the sedges.

Here we wait
and note, at the wood's edge
a new grave dug:
false flowers spewing their colour
on the muddy mound
and a new name burnishing
the ground:
a gull flies over.

     The earth has not shuddered
     nor have the heavens been sundered
     but a man has "been to the mountain-top"
     and we walk now, groping
     our sight shaken
     our voices broken.

Here we wait, while jays scream
in the pine-branches overhead
and a gull replies from far off
winging his way   solitary
over the flowing river.

Post-Operative Instructions

The hammer beating in   old doctrine
was mine   some lengths ago
but in this month of Czechoslovakia's fall
I meet my sickle too
am carved in a burning sweep
from breast to back
the canker taken out, they say—
a breathing wing made limp.

And as I walk again
fumble towards the sidewalk step
green intervals   hard road
and touch the roughness of oak bark
marvel at plane tree swirls and sworls,
my eye swings down
to see a beetle crawling up a leaf;
in his brown glitter, all my drops of sweat.

So put the small things first:
what hammer hammered and what sickle flayed
was useless:
you cannot flay a mountain-top.
Now put the small things first:
perceive the rowan-berry on the tree
and seize, as grandchild will
to roll it bouncing down the hill—
watch, eye squinting against sun
an eagle's glint, a heron's sudden fall.
Blot out machines, hear
only the crickets   ticking time, the sheer
of silence when the sea has sucked the shore.

Only this way will maps of Europe change
will tanks be undermined
and guns be tossed to hoist a cemetery—
old cars, old iron, scrap-heap dominance.
To move The Wall, we need a beaver's teeth,
an ant's persistent harrying;
to move mankind, use the mosquito's sting
and magnify his minute into centuries.

Birthday
(for Frank Bessai)

Every day
make the decision to die
I said to myself
and then
swung body through
the hospital doors
to visit you

Every day
hold the enamelled shell
(bright the October day)
high in greeting
ceremonial hello
sunlight flashing

Today it was flowers I brought
and named them over:
Here's poppy, here's anemone
and a brazen daisy
the last of the summer.
From your doped sleep the slow answer:
Where did you find them?
Flown ... perhaps ...
from coast to prairie?

Then I told you, no:
These I stole from the hospital
gardens. It's October!
But see how the petals
so sheer   so silken
are fresh as springtime.
> Out of your dream, the answer:
> *Dear . . . love . . . sweetheart . . .*
> *these are the colours I live with*
> *miracle colours . . .*

Bright the enamelled day!
On the edge of the hospital bed
I sat down beside you
neither living nor dying
but ready to go down
into your frost and gloom
holding between us this October shell:
an offering.

Woman

I am an old one
a nut gnarled
I feel myself shrivelling
inside
crack my shell
    and find in me
nothing:
    a film of dust.

Yet I am more, a shell:
within me when you sound
waves beat
    pebbles are sucked
      to roll downshore
the gravel sighs
    as your feet pass by.

and under the sea
    earth tremors shake
      rifts appear—
I am a shell, and more
    seething and splitting
      the ocean's floor . . .

Among Friends

Words speak
louder far
than actions—
words devour

Wyatt railed
at his tongue
for failing him
"always most cold"

I'd swallow mine, be dumb
if it would give me back
those words I madly made
too loudly flung

Carman and His Editors

I think my ghost would rise up in a rage
If they scissored *me*—or cut away a word!
And yet, I'm one of them! Have said, behind my breath,
"Come off it, Bliss, how could you write that line?
It spoils the whole." Yet why must We desire
you suited to our times?—pre-dated man?
For unlike Frost or Masters—Vachel Lindsay, even,
you could not make that leap; you could not leave
the wild romantic wood at the maples' turning.
Drugged by the sunlight on the log, you sat
letting caresses, women's voices, weave
a tapestry for wall, a Web for roof.
It is because you *did not care*, we have no right
to rip away a word, shatter a phrase.

Birthday

This body that delights in aging
secreting layers, edges, ridges
accumulating flesh for dust
this body's creaking joints and bulging veining
still feels the singe of sun
surrendering to the hand, the tongue—
at the still centre of a name
revives from ash and dross
creates a vortex where the words may toss
cinders above the flame.

Imprints

i

The seeds of my flowers
remained hidden so long
under permafrost
when sun released them
I scarcely believed
their colours

ii

Dawn pushes up
the usual sunflower
in a red tangle
of landscape

iii

The grass is circled by the children's love:
numb snow, so softly fallen
is marked with their geometry
ovals and squares—

until a hound, bounding with hoarse barks
distorts the angel shapes
buries their cries

iv

A silver moon has mapped
two elms upon the garden snow
two interlacing rivers
black
on white

But in the day
when the red lip of the sun
presses against dark limbs
no shadows show
what the night knew.

Ceremonial Journey

i

Sun's difference makes the difference
in people and in places.
From my west coast
where rock and water run
I see you bright
and armed in northern snow
crisp the crystals
dazzle your hair
my eyes.

But deeper at land's centre
where the continent
holds heat and people
there you glow
a taut bow poised—
you leap and run
engender excitement
from the flailing sun.

On fine free mornings you are found
in fettle for the searching word
in blaze of noon you stretch yourself
and flash your blade.
On cool gold afternoons
you flake the scales
of sun in tilting water
follow the sun's fish down
with darting laughter.
Night falls: assume your mask
under the cedars, become your shadow—
elusive now as loon's cry
over water
let fly your catapulting cry.

ii

And yet it is in darkness
where the differences dissolve
and tensions fly back into place
as branches close after a passer-by.
In darkness all the land lies similar
the rivers writing messages in a scrawled script
indecipherable except to you,
an airman now
steering your throbbing ship
through waves of night
across their language
flowing east and south.
Your read the alphabet of blotted lakes
and see the meaning in the sprawl
of Georgian Bay
black-fathomed by the moon;
and counties cut like paper-backs
printed by man and plow;
or racing eastward against time and self
you plunge through tumbled clouds
to the vast arm—
Saint Lawrence pouring words
into the yeasty sea.

The words are elevators towering above
curled rails and snouted trains;
the words are boats and barges
flags long flown
a thousand cars scuttling out at dawn
from country freeway to arterial doom.
But in Quebec the pink and purple farms
still hum their human messages:
the cattle brood on shady sides of night
until a man disturbs them with his pail—
shaking the milk-white light.

So it is day! the unity of land and night
splits in a thousand pieces.
You sheer off down the runway,
man again! throttle the flight.

Pin-pricked with dark
your numbed feet seek the soil
stumble upon daylight.

iii

See now our separateness.
Sun makes the difference
between your evening world
of sand and shore
and my gold-slanted noon.
You are absorbed with the tide's bore
Atlantic bite
and in your dreaming I hear Fundy roar.
Far west the shore I know:
Pacific's slow
soft plunge into the inlet's core.
Yet there's no difference!
both feel the common sense
of barnacle and fossil
salt and stone
and from this fiery fathering-place
we stand as one
bound on this rock
by the gold band of the sun.

Water Colours: Victoria

Beacon Hill

The trees demand some compliment
for someone planted streets of these—
a city father? One whose eyes had leapt
a hundred years ahead.
(The guide book does not mention him.)

But now, instead
of plotted grass, and paving stone
we move through aisles of sycamore,
the glossy-leaved—pale bones
gesticulating talk.
We turn a corner and as green
as Christmas sunk in summertime
the mountain ash (the rowan tree)
in a red rash of berry
feeds sparrows through the winter.
And honey locusts scoop another street
out of its primness, up to waving sky;
and running down a hill,
white birches wave their basketry;
most loving to the eye
arbutus lifts her red bole to the sky
and shakes a thousand ears of leaves
above the city's cars and cares.
Last, climbing to the park,
rock moss and barren grass
(air sea-blue, salt),
oak trees as intricate
as Chinese Ming, rove over rocks
set down their tough umbrellas
in the city's heart.

Parliament Buildings

The best exhibit is outdoors:
sequoia, a cedar of Lebanon
red-wooded wisdom calling up
California and Captain Cook
and Spanish galleons billowing their sails;
and long before she heard the gullible voice
assessing and surveying, she was witness of
the killer whale harpooned upon the shore,
Haida war cry
medicine of prayers.

Her branches point within
where in an archive neatly tucked away
John Jewett's story—seized by savages:
who now so sweetly civilized and tamed
on the carved cedar pole
sell to the tourists for a song
their private history.

Of her own history
sequoia breathes no word.

Hotel Garden

In the walled garden where
standard roses (shot with candytuft)
flaunt their heritage of blood,
Verbena and Sweet William mask the earth,
feeding the eye;
while lavender's faint breath
nourishes the air.

The shady walks are garlanded
with girls, their skirts like upturned parasols;
they whirl their carousels
stepping upon the cautious paving stones
(rough earthen plates in emerald grass)—
their soft balloons starting the summer air
parting enamelled flowers, stiff porcelain.

Convention

Into the street poured
the Witnesses all overawed
with the libations of the Lord:
their throaty choruses
vibrating still
against grey wall,
against green hill.

Into my veins poured
the liquid action of your words;
transfusion to be stored
against the gloom of winter days:
testimony of tossing flowers,
full-throated colours shouting praise!

Sonnet for the Times

So many duties we have falllen heir to
responsibilities and reins
for father and for son; but also for
the holy ghost we call the human spirit
flowering through the chinks
of crumbling wall, torn pavement
only to become a metal flower
bombarded into icy cold by *strontium ninety*

And yet the secret formula exists, wherewith
to turn the metal into green again
and see it leaf; to pull a silky blade
of grass to its small utmost of resilience
more tough than nylon—feel the spring of it!
and glossier than glass.
The formula exists in our own minds
and must be wrenched:
"In dreams begin responsibilities."

High Rise

From 8 a.m. when figures scurry
and movement moves
I watch the great arm
arching the universe
and am not moved!
struck dumb and impotent
by that ambivalent cross
I watch, still mesmerized
to see the modern bridgework turning
the cables gripped in place
the men as midgets
obediently flying

     and I lie down!
     hide it from my eyes
     although I know
     I'm going to beg a "place"
     in that new block
     and spend old age
     on a soft bed
     howling for hard meadows
        weeds   stones   clods
     and a smothering sheet
        of daisies.

Hibiscus

On a Saturday afternoon
when everyone adult has been to the bars
and home to the long, langorous luncheon
served by the barefooted
white-coated
black man;
when the youngsters (white)
spindly-legged and shrill
have been sucked into the 20th-century cinema

At such a time
have you ever sat in your car
and listened to the sounds that remain left over, as it were
from the morning's fray?
A car in the distance, growling into high gear,
a bird-like screech of brakes
and, off-stage,
an inconsequential toot-toot of a hooter?
Onstage, on the walk,
dry leaves falling from the jacaranda tree
scuttle across the pavement chuckety-chuck
for there is a breeze blowing this swinging September day
and the tossing mauve blossoms of the jacaranda tree
swim upon blue air
while from the hibiscus hedge,
shielding the blaze from the sidewalk,
surge soft flames.

Voices are passing—
Indian children
two Africans
on a bicycle.

Leda Again

The hand that warms my belly
Is the sun's
He thrusts my legs apart and strokes the hair
Undoes me on a bed of moss and crushed sea pinks
And rolls me over sweet again
Pricks my flesh green again—

Writhing, the body breaks.

The body breaks. As bread is torn, devoured,
The body yields and shakes
The bones dissolve in moss and stone
And rock's rib shapes the spine.

I lie, accepted: by the earth,
By humming wind whose sound
Tree-sifted, shifts its tone
To underpass the silences;
I lie, accepted: by the clouds
That change their angles in the lake
Sever their shadows, re-unite;
And by the wild hawk hovering
Who veers, sun-blinded, from my body's light.

The hand that takes me knows me at day's end
Stone still, all glowing gone—
And yet, pulsing within
Fire's embryo at the bone.

I KEEP PREPARING:
THE 1970S

I keep preparing
my death
re-arranging
the pillow
opening and closing
envelopes
re-filing
folders
I keep rehearsing
the last words to be inserted
on the typewriter ribbon

Jack on the Telephone Beanstalk

O my wild left-turner
since when have you become
such a happy bourgeois?

Madly I could love you
you paranoic schizophrenic
waking me
2 a.m.
"I'm dying"
forcing me out
on a fogged night
round and round
the raped city

O my wild left-turner
you've learned now
all the RIGHT
turns
and what can I do but applaud
clap for an admirable
"adjustment to social stress?"
Yet I long to disbelieve!

If anything ever mattered it was you
YOU
falling out of a taxi and breaking your glasses
stabbing at store windows
it was you, coming bloody to my bed
crying "salve!"

As I see you now
calmly taking up fishing   canoeing
even photography and chess
I applaud your remarkable
resilience

but in my lone   sky tower
I still listen
for that quivering voice
climbing   note over note
the telephone ladder

Out of the cradle . . .

OUT OF THE CRADLE

To lie naked
among rocks   dry grasses
to let the juice
of the old rejuvenator

ENDLESSLY

enter my bones
bless my skin
to cheer for the fructation
of blackberries   over picket fences
and hummingbirds   in honeysuckle

ROCKING

to give my approval
to striated sky
cloud whiffs
to tolerate, even
the raucous crow
backtalking

to concentrate
on the toddler's effort   towards
     language

OUT OF THE CRADLE

the naming—the noun—*stone   pinecone
car   plane   sun*
and hear his astonishment
(after seizing too fast
a fluttering moth)
the verb:
it hurts

ENDLESSLY

to wonder how my body
could be hurt   reviled
or any woman's body
just because she's growing
older
and how the young men poets
with their steel-fenced egos
would face up to Lawrence
or even to
that young love
who came to me as a person
with gentleness

ROCKING

his mind also making a fine incision
honed to perception

And how can such things be—
these other
suicidal cut-offs?
when the the grass leaf
which Whitman (stealing the sun)
extolled and glorified
the grass leaf springs back under my hand
as a penis extending
or a moth's wing
spurting

OUT OF THE CRADLE

into bright air

ENDLESSLY ROCKING

Savour of Salt

The eye needs tears
my doctor says—
to be healthy.
But if, after sixty years
one cannot weep?
Go down to the sea
like your father
bathe in sea salt
water
and bring a bottle of it
home
for the stiff winter.
I remember my father
a strong swimmer
eyes drying
in the sun.

McLuhan Criticized

The Greeks had the advantage
of never seeing their stars
in the flesh
(Hollywood could not be visited)
therefore the imagination
created its own pornography
and art

Today we leave it all to celluloid:
the whims and cavortings
of our gods and goddesses
offer no instruction—
a diversion only
for the loneliness
of the outdistanced
masses

Flight 403

Though I was certain
we recognized each other
I could not speak:
the flashing fire
between us
fanned no words

In the airport circle where
the baggage tumbled
all my jumbled life
fumbled
to find the one sweet place
recognizable, fine
the clothing stuffed and duffled
labelled mine

And over across the circle   saw your
dark hair, piercing eyes
lean profile, pipe in mouth

You move. You seem to dance
towards me
and suddenly you stand beside me
calm
without surprise

I cannot tell
what country you are from.
We recognize each other
and are dumb

Your hand   your hand
tense on your pipe
your final look
a soft blow
forever on my mind

The Invasion

I woke to hear a small one running
overhead: the rain.
After the white and fiery day
the swords of hoarfrost crossed at play
and every cedar in the slashed wood
supine and stiff in a white shroud
geometry going mildly mad
in mirrors of ice
caught between stump and stump—
a "whiteprint" on a map of countries caught
only in fragments (as mind's buildings are
held in shape by the smooth-gloved
white-pricked weather)—

I woke to hear a small one running:
she washed the winter from the wood.
The tiny mosses, crystallized
(printed on rock in miniatures)
were laved in sorriness
back to the brown habit;
and the crisp apples on the stiff tree
shook off their icy filagree;
a junco swooping for his suet
lost his hard beak in sudden slush.
        (I heard the Athenian hunter tell again
        of how they came in rowboats to the shore
        and on the beach took cover, thence to shoot
        a thousand metres up, the mountain goats
        shaggy and hoar with frost
        who fed on stone and rock
        and leaned a head too near the upland edge
        and so were shot . . .
        if shot well, they would fall
        to the beach for luck.)
I woke to hear a small one running there:
rain devouring winter.

On Cleaning a Chicken
(for A. M. Klein)

Remembering your marvellous
dawn-cracking rooster

I wish I didn't have to
cut off this head, these claws
pull out these guts
grey oily strings
and bleeding heart-shaped things
only to make a meal
and to wish
on a wishbone.

Interior Landscape
(for Roy Kiyooka)

How then
   do you perceive the butterfly?
I perceive it
   as poetry itself
entering this window to flutter
    in orange-yellow-brown
       delight
yet trapped!   striving forever for light
barred by the barren man-made glass
deprived of air   sky   freedom to fly
and breathe,

Dear poetry. stop flut   ter
ing   descend   be calm
    hover   my darling
pause
however many the hands
that seek to trap you   and send
your body out of the window
fast—
they fear your wings!
they will not touch   but twist
paper
shove paper bats to flush you out
from that blare glass
glare ice where you   exhausted
flap

Only a man with wings   sandalled
  (he, Roy)
       can capture your anxiety
        and calm it down
look how he seizes you
   firm on the rightmost wing
and sends you, pling—
out of the window
into arms of air.

my moth.   brown butterfly.
soul trembling.   touching.   there
and there.
the verb to be: linking
the mouth: waiting   for the song
the moth:
dancing

forever here   and here.

Not

So we walked up and down the street
wondering
why the meeting didn't start
not daring to ask the lone policeman
swinging his baton   up and down
pacing   the opposite
way

In the end nobody came
there was no meeting
not even between us
not daring to say hello to the cop
not knowing
what he knew

Then the bomb went off
and shot diamonds of glass
from the jewelry store
splintering our eyes

The cop was blown up.

We stay now
in the dark forever.

The Children in the Car

They're like
my nagging thoughts
that claim attention
my right elbow
as I drive

and when they press too close
or ask queer questions
perhaps I'll turn my head
one movement wrong
and the car takes over

brakes then
screams
open the window

explain   explain

how do you explain?

Retirement in Victoria

In pairs
linked by scarves and raincoats
plastic galoshes
old ladies parade
to the Drugstore
for ease from that nagging rheumatic joint
to the Bank
for cashing the government bonanza
to the Post-Office
for one 8-cent stamp please
and to talk with the frizzy-haired
dyed blonde postmistress
a minor angel
God's listener
to every tenant's woe
(while the customers queue up).

"I hear Mrs. Pimlico
has gone to Los Angeles for the winter"
"But what's wrong with *our* climate?
Mild, of course
and instead of that white prairie stuff—
RAIN!"
"But it's the wind I dread
that wind, destroying ships
tearing the soul from sailors"

Sometimes there's a lone old man
doing his constitutional
proffering sweets
to children
as he walks along Cook to Pandora
and back again
but often
there are couples with canes
he, she
painfully dependent on each other's moods
and whims

coming to great decisions
in the grocery store
as to which cut of beef is cheaper

and sometimes
in full view of the passers-by
lashing out, "I won't, I won't!"
hate of their chains
hate of each other.

I'll tell you
(if you ask me)
there's pity and fear
and
FRIGHT
in the attic lodgings
the damp basement apartments
when no son or daughter
lifts up the telephone
to say hello.

The Interrogation

"Concrete poetry is devoted to objects.
No symbolism may intrude."

Who is the other person in the room?
There is no other person in the room.
Who is it you are talking to?
Emptiness.
What has replaced people?
Objects have replaced people.

I am an olding woman
alone with objects—
but thank god they breathe
daisies   growing grasses   sea birds

Strip me   and
search me.
I am not a drug addict.
I have no secrets.

Barometer Falling

Our age is all
as Eliot and Yeats decreed
our age is all
rage; rape

Fun and folly
the lowest possible intelligence
interviewed on radio
as "interesting"

Unheard is the
pure searching thought
furious fire
cleaving the white flower of truth

Inevitably we see them fall:
Churchill, Roosevelt, Stalin
Mao—
The world's witches have concocted
no magic power
against the dissolution of man.

Prairie Flight

In Canada
no need for abstract painters.
Farmers have shaped
with their hands, their boots, their horses' hooves
last, with tractors
a bright geometry imposed
on buffalo bones

Staring at land
only for wheat and hay
with the curled rivers and lakes
sore thumbs
right in their way
those silent carvers of the land
send messages they never see.

Annunciation

If I opened that door
onto the dark
I'd touch such mystery
I'd be transformed

But here I walk among the hard rocks
the boiling sea
deformed

The foetus within me cries
to find a new
way out
perfectly formed

Three Kingdoms
(for Charlotte Brontë)

It was a fatal thing
that having borne books,
given birth to so many creative flights,
wrestling with angels,
you turned away at forty
to be Victorian,
to be married.
On your honeymoon
"It is a strange and different thing"
you wrote your old friend, Ellen.
In due course,
ill abed near nine months,
you gave birth to the dead child
and then
you gave yourself up.

It is given to women to choose,
even in our time:
but there are not three kingdoms.
She may have two
but never three.

Gabe
(for Carol Bolt)

Say that I have to say it
tell me
it's all second hand
Your grief and pain
(my Métis friend)
     sifted through me
a blank white screen

Your fantasies shiver
upon my body's shaking frame
I follow you where you dream
of being Riel, Dumont,
of climbing into that green heaven
where the white man's rule
is shrunk, shriven.
     Driven,
you are driven
by phantasmagoric dreams
fog falling
clouds obscuring
as you steer
that super-powered heaven-geared
You Drive car
into your own drunk haven: oblivion

Tell me I do not know
I cannot understand
I'm second-hand
Then kiss me!
Break your body into 1000 elements
of energy,
splash me with joy,
aliens too long in this melting
we are stripped bare
have become one
     here
       there

The Bethune Wind

There is no such thing as silence
                    —John Cage

The Bethune wind
is March-splintered
howls across the campus
snarls up the angles of buildings
cries DOOM DOOM
as we gather to commemorate
Spain.

Inside the carpeted halls
(hushed spaces)
counter-sounds reply:
jazz in the Pub
shouts from racketeers
hitting the celluloid
pong   ping
                yin   yang
And somewhere in a rotunda
a Spanish voice vibrates
in vowels and syllables
caressing his country
binding us to his pain.

Time Zone

When I most vividly think of you
it is early morning
you are lying asleep
two hours behind me
on the west coast.

Your left arm is curled
under the bedclothes
waiting for my head
to rest there
yet not waiting—
holding and having.

I like to imagine
that fire of my thinking
somehow hovers
an aureole over
your dreaming eyes.

Iconoclast

Stuck in the mud
      of your own upbringing
reaching to "the outward and
        visible sign"—
but grace seeks for you
      sighs for you
humility calls within

You have led yourself
      up to the border
where revolution explodes
but you turn back
      disguised in clown's clothing
slip under the ropes
      to the trodden roads

You prance round
      like a dandy
in your fine bourgeois clothes
but who are you
      longing to be truly?
a hippy without shoes
an anarchist without a country
a poet without truths.

I, Happiest

I don't politick:
I hammer
tap tapping lightly
sometimes I bludgeon
but I don't worm myself
into the body politic
to feed my ego
and destroy others

I, happiest
sitting serene by the river
toes tap touching
the silver water
if it flows
(as it will)
into death's dark

I, happiest
to have sent one spark
ignited for a flash
of time
upon the expanding
universe

Ars Poetica

i

Words have
        no mortality
exist in innocence

handled well
        can perform miracles
gently massaging
        the heart

ii

Ralph,
on my first undistracted evening
in Ottawa
I heard you airing
your Russian travelogue
        historical architectural
spiritual journey
but *yours*
not Moscow's.

Thus do poets thrive!
We are vultures feeding
on the remains of man
in order to stay alive
and fly.

iii

One feather
winging its way down
graces the air

three or four more
set the mind floating

but a thousand feathers
Ugh!
a choking pillow.

iv

There's a wind out there
suffers no silence gladly:
we harness him with words—
he likes that whip
yet
like snowballs secretly
laden with ice
can strike the eye
blind

Comrade

Flight of delight
songs, ravings
        syllables
of thought
arrows sent side
along side
into the body of the world,
laughter shooting straight
the moon our bullseye
        and the sun
our lying in—
O long lost comrade
in these dark times
we will meet ever hereafter
apart again
send new shafts,
reversible absurdities
of word play,
eternal bouts of laughter.

Caution: To Nadine

You ask
(it seems naïvely)
all the leading questions
and I answer
(it seems naïvely)
as closely as possible
And yet between us
we writhe with evasions.

You do not wish to probe
nor I to be probed
yet our mutual poetic concern
for the truth
creates
this stutter

Moving Around

When from full face morning
sun beams out at left of the pine tree
till noon, when he appears beneficent
heading for his home
We know
        it's only ourselves turning
        our world shifting its gaze
the way, as children
we sat in a train at the station
and watched ourselves moving—
but it was only the train on the next track
shunting backwards

As clouds also
deceive us with their motion
seeming arrested
while we fly on
        And sometimes I have seen your face
        caught in a trance—
        then it is I who am moving
        on the tragic stage
        in a drugged
        dance.
        It is I, distorted,
        moving around
        bound.

The Continuum
(in memory: Pat Lowther, October, 1975)

The first snow
falls—through naked elms and oaks
rain wraiths quick crystalled,
shaped—
falls upon olive-green water
this secretly flowing
ongoing
river.

Secretly flowing
your life
chopped off at prime
victim of violent hate
but secretly flowing
your body in the salt
water (your loved Pacific)
ebbs in and out
with the tide
one with the crabs   clams   oysters
octopi   you wrote about
crustaceans on the ancient rock.

You said of Pablo
(O all your "Letters to Neruda"
predict death, predict life)
called him *dark jewel of history*
a seed patient us time

And here again
as the snow (by Riel's river)
resumes, soft shroud,
I feel your poems falling clean
upon our living
alive with your pleading,
incisive tongue,
untarnished vision—
O may your words
return   return
to heal our griefs,
seal cicatrice,
emblaze for us
the dark gulf
of being.

All the Good Things

So many of my days spent
fulminating against the bad things:
landgrabs, collusion, pollution,
decimation of children—
so many of my days
wasted in fury
at what we've turned the world into—

But suddenly
moments bloom like an unwatched
secret flower
Suddenly women move onto the streets
demanding peace in Belfast
Suddenly a voice from Newfoundland
a woman painter
tells of a sailing trip to a wild
    lone island
And suddenly a small boy
cuddles his puppy.
In a Winnipeg Art Gallery, paintings,
faces from the world's past
gleam out at us from Moscow
with mod haircuts and wearing
blue weather-beaten trousers:
the *same* faces—1670 or 1976!

And suddenly I wonder:
am I only a sentimental old woman?
Or is there a tune there, twining
my frantic past
with your assured future?

Rush Hour

If men   women
have chosen to slither,
slugs in steel traps on wheels,
coiling, uncoiling—
turn on the music!
Schubert or Mozart
or even rock
could stir an earthworm's heart?
could set us on a meditative swing
beyond the glued, slow oozing forward
traffic pains
into that realm
where we truly belong:
under the sea, with whales,
under the earth's crust,
with moles and earthworms
into the air
where the meadowlark imprints
his solitary song.

Canadian

When the blizzard strikes Ottawa
every machine gives up.
"All flights cancelled."
"Trains behind schedule."
"Buses struggle through."
"Cars stuck and abandoned."

The mutely standing
mutely waiting civil servants
bunched in twenties, thirties
blocking street corners
have little of their pioneer fathers'
gumption!

A few set out, grimly walking
and bump into ME—
just a little old lady ploughing on
under the only umbrella in town,
white as a dying dandelion
and laughing.

The Critics

It's not all praise and blame
we're after
That's too easy
It's to find a thought or action
we wish we had captured
and owned
—the four-leaf-clover
that as children
(hunt as we might
in a daze of grass)
we never found.

Home Town

The wind at Portage and Main
was a collector's item:
"the coldest spot in Canada!"
In winter
a knife between the knees
a box on the ears;
In spring
fistfuls of crocus air
pelted;
In summer's dripping heat
a devil, whirling skirts;
In fall
honeycoloured
spattering oak leaves
ash   aspen
blown from nowhere
down.

The wind at Portage and Main
is not there anymore:
banned!
They've pumped him underground
caged him in a stifling mall
neon lighted   computer weighted
man tall

And no one's allowed to walk anymore
across Portage and Main—
no one at all.
Verboten.
Passage interdit.
Trespassers will be prosecuted.

Martyrs, Anonymous
(for Allisan)

Sometimes when in pain
she imagined herself a female christ
forced to stand against a wall
with the arrows flailing

If only they don't hit my eyes
she thought
so they aimed straight
piercing cleanly each eye

And darkness
swallowed the world

I Keep Preparing

I keep preparing
my death
re-arranging
the pillow
opening and closing
envelopes
re-filing
folders
I keep rehearsing
the last words to be inserted
on the typewriter ribbon

But it won't happen
as expected
it will be like this dream
I wake from:
shaggy cat hissing in the brown grass
and my dog, leaping over the stile
to attack—
she reels and falls back
stiff as a porcupine

No preparation was needed
for the thunderbolt.

In the Cupboard

Vivaldi and Telleman
come through on the fading
FM
only as ghosts of song
squeaking skeletons

Now breaking in
your voice, on the telephone
Hellololo
hails from a far century
a foreign space

remote as music vibrant once
its frame still there
but the flesh frayed
the garments long outworn:
they dash and dare
all colours gone.

Action de Grâce
(written upon Ralph Connor's desk)

It is
a thanksgiving
to be back here in your house
looking out through the bared
autumn oaks
to the Assiniboine's grey-brown
flowing water

Nevermind
the Maryland bridge
and its suffocating roar
nevermind the obstructions.
There are black squirrels
leaping through these branches
there are jays, juncoes
a thousand winged things
still living on man's edges

Nevermind how
man mindlessly cringes

There are spirits rising
candles lighted
held in procession
there is a solemn
exaltation offered
to the season's
lightning changes
snow   wind   incredible
melting sun

Nevermind nevermind
those who gave up the ghost
always there is one left
whose will
alters the equation.

Prose and Poetry

Beyond the poems
there's so much to say
the poems go downward
that's it
locked underground

the other impetus
a net of words
flung upward
attempts to snare
the whole damn
unlistening
sky.

Thoughts after Meditation

We can shut out the light
the chair, the table,
close the eyes,
seal the lips tight,
the ears also
plugged against sound

But O how to close out words
once language has
     seized the brain?

The babe, having struggled
     to speak,
to make words work
"Come"   "go"
"love me"
"eat"
the babe should be taught also
how to close words off,
toss away toys,
shut poetry out
to register only
the script of silence.

Roomers

The attic love-life
of the girl across the rooftops
impinges upon
my solitary housekeep:
when she cries out
      too ecstatically
I rattle the dishes
or move from kitchen to bathroom
and flush the toilet

For a while, silence—
then laughter slivers
and slices the airways—
and, I too
can't help laughing

Surreal

I am in a dream
within a wood
not able to move,
become a watcher.

But you throw the ball of fire
look!
I become a catcher,
hold in my gnarled hand
the key to nature.
Turn it over
and winter flowers
on the jack-frost pane.
Turn it twice
and a green rain falls
dissolving all your fears.
Turn it thrice
and you pound the earth
with your body
demanding, demanding
the green forces of summer.
In the fourth season
you walk through fire
eternally turn
into the flames, driven

out of this drouth
find haven,
heaven.

A Stranger   But No Ghost

You are not hearsay   nor
a man I merely dreamed of
you appeared
were real

It was not a game   merely
your loving me
each one needed
mending

Nothing is buried now
though bones and flesh
arms   arms
are gone to earth

Nothing is buried when
the fire furies on
eyes flash   and the tongue
talks miracles

To Robbie Burns
(from one of his mistresses)

You are the ghost I live with.
Because you are alive
I talk and talk
    the day's delights
            the night's disasters   over
knowing you're here
your ear receptive
somewhere
your voice responding   aye

        And were you dead and gone
        would I be prone
        to open up my heart
        and cut the truth
        in careful pieces for you?

You are the ghost, living or dying!
Here   or gone
in you my life takes on
a darling double—
if you are god, I wait:
and if the devil
I can give him too
a devil of trouble.

The Woman Syndrome
(for Annie)

Time took me unawares
for I was laughing
it seemed I had a mirthful mind
and was beloved
even (it seemed)
I was the eternal woman
sought for and never captured
herself complete

Time taught me
in the full-length mirror
I was only bulges   creases
a crimped back and a creased neck
a belligerent belly

> Who am I
> anyway?
> body or person?
> person or woman?

No man will tell me

ANYTHING GOES: THE 1980s

Above all
a poem records speech:
the way it was said
between people   animals   birds
a poem is an archive for our times

Old Woman

I walk
uninhibited
yet inhabited   withal
by ancestors

Norman
    Saxon
        Gael
grandfathers and grandmothers
alert to the times
country gentry   farm hands
painters   architects   poets
Plymouth Brethren   dyed in the wool
Anglicans   self-proclaimed
radicals
all simmering together
to create me
and my progeny
those bursting forth grandchildren
their unforeseen directions

I walk
uninhibited
careless of the world's glance—
these gnarled bones bind me downwards:
but in the mind
I dance. I dance!

Pause

Is it a sudden thing:
the bud opening into flower
at the first blink of sun?

It has taken a year
of the seed's life
to erupt this way

And I also am new born
suddenly today!
yet slowly
through seventy years

Willow Island (Lake Winnipeg)
(for David Arnason)

White pelicans light here, where first
Icelandic refugees sighted the land
and sighed for safety.
It is safe now, for birds and men:
the long neck of willow bush and sand
windswept, with fish for the taking
six feet from shore, at the end of the rod.
It is safe now for man, for woman:
in the midst of our nettled fever
of grab and gain and profit-making
an oasis of water, wind, bulrushes swishing—
we are children again, crusoes exploring reason
ingenuity against blind cunning
survivors against
our cruel gift for killing.

The Tipster

You'll just fall asleep
        one day
the medicine man said
and wake up
dead

Okay by me, I saluted him
okay and thanks
as long as I don't wake up
ill or addled
crippled or straddled
as long as I can shrink
clean as a newborn babe
and burrow down under
with earth for cover:
no dreams   no food   no drink
nor tears or laughter
an artifact—
for the hereafter

Letter in Praise of Prairie

This lake speaks
louder far than ocean—
my lake   your ocean

I try to tell you
in overlapping ways—
waves—
how water sometimes sounds all day
all night
heavier than the sough of wind
through trees
(though often these
are talking too)

How at midnight now
I wake from a dream of you
to know the beach is here
sand and shingle
stones mossy green
and monsters smoothed to boulders
by spring's restless ice—
the beach stretching forever
north   south
a milky sky stretching forever
to the other unseen shore

I try to tell you
how space is, here:
more of it   than among
your evergreen crowd   of jewels
island upon island

Sometimes you hear
storms frothing—
high wind and rain
but never the forked tongues
flashing through midnight poplars
the thrashing shock
of thunder—
never the day's unpeopled water
skimmed over by a survey of wings
white pelicans

Yes, eagles inhabit both our skies!
hawks   and the ebb and flow
of gulls
blue butterflies in beach grass
sandpipers' jerky darts
and you, O yes
joyful   your senses swimming
with surge of whales
sea otters   dolphins
cavorting northward

But it's the space
unsmothered
I am trying to embrace you with
white billows of cloud
untrammeled
travelling all heaven high
my arms   wings
sailing on air
freer than they were
where you abide—
tide-ridden
    curled in a cove
            boarded round
in a secret garden.

The Still World

The still world of trees
holds us in trance
We could urge them to root down
wisely   slowly
utter acceptance into
the inner spaces
of our hearts
our consciousness
We could urge them to implant
upon our human egos
something of silence
                          communion
                                certainty:
"If man does not destroy us
we offer ourselves
for his selective gardening"

The trees will never rise up and defy
even though we assassinate
their holdings

Osmosis

The clothes he wore
hang in the cupboard
shape of his angular elbows
the lop-sided shoulder

Against the tweed jacket
I lean, scenting tobacco.

The great thing is to get
all my senses in action
circling   listening
as a dog sniffs the grass
for remembrance

Soon I will hear the voice
echoing from the cupboard
Soon I will grow
new eyes.

Self on TV

My screwed eyes
fixed, plated
    smile
and chunky cheeks
are so unlike
the way I feel

Myself, girl in woods
hugging birch trees
by moonlight—
a nymph appearing
disappears—
aware of world's woe
my country's summer
and its glittering snow
aware of voices
      calling and singing
"I am a woman. Human.
I am alive . . . I know."

My shrunken face
my body's wretched
      stance
a challenge to someone:
"Madam, stand up
stand up and dance!"

A Soft Answer to Borges

What vast world
shaking its fist at us
or turning its back
has to be caught
            and kissed
sucked in and
            swallowed
(made visible)
dimensioned down
to man?

What world he strode in
thinking the circled path
was his to play in
that rest—that thundering sky
tempestuous sea
fathomable
      touchable?

He now has to seize
the void in his hands
shaped to his mouth
and through that horn of immensity
bellow out
his defiant song

January Snow: A Letter

I am so at home with winter
You couldn't even
lure me into those Bahaman
Jamaican highlands islands
the lush curled succulent
Hawaiian sands
Where Winnipeggers fly IN DROVES
to forget Christmas
to forget their bounds.
I need Christmas
and icebound New Year's trees
cushioned in whole reefs
of snow
where squirrels burrow
I need to skate on ice
with no escape
just facing up together
to near blizzard weather
"take care
get home
as soon
as you can"
It's not survival
but revival:
the kitchen and the kitchen stove
the kettle's hum
somehow someway
mon patrimoine—
       a coming home

Jove's Daughter

The father seduced her; not by love
but by the secret summons of the bone
that builds brain targets, knocks them down
and leaves the child immured, alone.

The father seduced her; his sin rings
round all her circular circuitings.
Not in the flesh did he
take her to bed
but in the embrace implied
the declaration never said
—Bind yourself round me—
(under the glove, the lead)
and she complied;
till her lover slit at the vine
slashed as she cried.

But every lover following, knew
she was not his, but Jove's shrew.

Mending

We build relationships
    with bits of tin
oddments of string, cord, coil.
You split wood
while I light fire   brew soup—
the cracked bowl fascinates
the handle off the cup—
Can these be fixed?
Sometimes!
We both look up at the cedar wall
where my rare Italian plate   shines
blue and green welded by you
old world clay against virgin forest.
Things tie us together.

Entering

Entering your world
I come as sister
to sit   a listener
learning new lettering
new numbers—
I put away in a hidden trunk
every anxiety that encumbers

Your voice and accent
dominate my mind
as though you held and steered
the pencil in my hand

Epiphany
(for Gwendolyn)

And suddenly
from an invitation to come
to my room to talk

Suddenly

we were all one

girl from Germany
man from America
girl from Italy
philosopher from Ottawa
literary historian
doctoral candidate
and you—poet—
Gwendolyn
So giving of your wisdom

Suddenly we were
      all an orchestra

against nuclear war

death of our planet

Suddenly
      from our diversity
words linked us
in a ring of stars

Anything Goes

A poem can be many things
in miniature:
a short story   about people
a photograph
a surreal landscape
and perhaps
an instant of ecstacy?

A small sermon
a prophetic warning
sometimes a wild experiment with music
and sound
or just   a fable

Above all
a poem records speech:
the way it was said
between people   animals   birds
a poem is an archive for our times

That is why   NOW   today
a poem must cry out
against war

AFTERWORD

by Di Brandt

It is fitting to celebrate the lifetime achievement of Dorothy Livesay, Canada's *grande dame* of poetry, with this retrospective of previously unpublished and uncollected works.

The mere fact of this archive's existence, the size and scope of it, is eloquent testimony to the unwavering commitment Livesay made to poetry through the more than six decades of her writing life. Writing poems clearly preceded any plans for publication. The exuberance of voice and spirit which we so admire in her work is reflected in the largesse of an archival file of this quality: an unreserved arena of self-expression and creative exploration, and a rich reserve to draw on for revision or inclusion in future collections.

No doubt this archive also bears witness to the difficulties of being a woman writer in Canada in this century: forced to be otherwise employed and often itinerant due to a dearth of permanent residencies for writers; and having to negotiate the double demands of a professional woman in the public arena, and a wife or consort, mother and grandmother domestically. The price of creativity was perhaps a lack of organization of her affairs; it is startling to imagine how much more Livesay might have achieved in her already stellar career had she received the kind of ongoing professional and personal support she clearly deserved.

A collection of this sort is unusual enough to raise interesting questions: Which of these poems were intended for book publication in their present form in Livesay's mind? How does this collection change her *oeuvre*, posthumously, without her consent, so to speak? To what extent should we read these poems as background material, and to what extent as completed text? What new information can these relatively unedited poems shed on her poetic project, and what authority do they carry?

Like most writers, Livesay sometimes worried about her literary reputation. The sheer span of her writing career, from the twenties through the war and postwar years, through the turbulent sixties and on to the nineties, meant that she was engaging constantly with new literary forms and ideas, while passionately defending and developing her own aesthetic. She was a formidable presence in the Canadian literary scene: younger poets newly influenced by the Black Mountain school or feminist theory or poststructuralism, and waving their first literary manifestoes, were bound to encounter Livesay, blunt, skeptical, confrontational, but *there*, lively, curious, alert, on top of things.

She possessed the long view, a nearly century-long commitment to a particular kind of writing: socially conscious, spare, imagist, forthright, and erotically charged, inspired by modernism and a politically minded upbringing, and fuelled by a fierce curiosity and desire for creative independence. At the same time she had an amazing ability to recreate herself poetically over and over in response to social and intellectual changes around her, and her own life experiences as a woman. In this way she had a powerful effect on younger writers, who might be attached to a particular theory as they began writing, but couldn't help being impressed and challenged by the tenacity and adaptiveness of her long-term vision, and her bold, clear-eyed manner.

I first met Livesay in 1984, as a member of the newly formed feminist editorial collective of *Contemporary Verse* 2, the magazine she founded in Winnipeg during her Writer-in-Residency at the University of Manitoba in 1975. (The title was itself a nod to an earlier magazine, *Contemporary Verse*, founded in Vancouver in 1941 by Livesay, Anne Marriott, Doris Ferne, and Floris McLaren, and edited by Alan Crawley.) The other members of our collective were Jane Casey, Jan Horner, and Pamela Banting. Livesay was impressed to see all this new editorial energy connected with the magazine, and profoundly mistrustful of our direction, influenced as we were by the new continental theory, just then being translated into English. And indeed our first editorial, penned by Pamela Banting, made extravagent claims to "new critical strategies," such as "reader-response criticism, deconstruction, the pleasure of the text, odysseys to explore the constitution of a self in language, etc." and "inquiries into genre or the gender politics of language."[1]

---

1   Pamela Banting, "blurred mirrors and the archaeology of masks," *Contemporary Verse* 9.1 (1985) 6.

I was a little scared of Livesay and her critical eye and tongue, and avoided her after that, though I continued to read and admire her work. But after a wonderful reading she gave in Winnipeg several years later, I couldn't help myself, and ran up to her, gushing my thanks. Who are you? she said. And thus began nearly a decade of friendship, in which she regularly called me when she came through town, for coffee and a rousing literary chat. I valued these visits highly. I called her my literary grandmother, cross-generational muse of ecstatic self-expression and keen-eyed observation. And she thought of me also as a kind of daughter or granddaughter, kindred rebel against staid convention, a partner in *caring*.

I know Livesay had similar friendships with women across Canada, and this kind of blunt, sharp-eyed mentoring from a veteran woman artist to younger women strikes me now as generous beyond words, and inestimable in value. You can hear it in her writing also, a growing sense of responsibility toward younger women, protecting, encouraging, passing on secrets, challenging them to help "SAVE OUR WORLD," to "explode the universe / with the power of colour music words."[2] She enjoyed, as she put it less reverently in another poem, the opportunities and reversals of old age, finding herself one of

> these 5 old ladies . . . trans-generationists
> who take on
> the motorcycle gang
> the hold-up guy
> kidnappers and hi-jackers
> and simply bomb the town
> with the power of their ten arms.[3]

I realize now her poetics and sensibility have had a much greater influence on me over the years than I could have understood then: her acute sense of social justice, her love of plain, irreverent speech, her gift for precise, evocative images, her passionate connection to landscape, her commitment to erotic liberation, and especially inde-

---

2   Dorothy Livesay, "A Hug for Beth," *Feeling the Worlds: New Poems* (Fredericton: Goose Lane, 1984) 24-25.

3   Livesay, "Salute to Monty Python," *Feeling the Worlds* 40.

pendence as a woman, her desire for love, community, relationship. I go back and read my favourite poems by her over and over: "Green Rain," "The Uninvited," "Salute to Monty Python," "The Unquiet Bed." She opened so many doors for people, for readers and artists and particularly women. We are just beginning to understand her looming stature in Canadian letters, and will be documenting it for some time to come.

I think Livesay would be pleased to see this "archive for our times" in print, gratified to be recognized and remembered in this way by readers willing to pay attention to work she cared about but could not find time to organize. And delighted to find herself being recreated yet again, by ardent students of her craft, at the end of this century, after a lifetime of personal and aesthetic "epiphanies" and revisions of her self and her world.

Certainly her readers will be happy to discover the strength and range of these newly published poems. Many of them are gems indeed, and will surely be included in future anthologies of Livesay's work. We can all be grateful to the editor, Dean J. Irvine, for his careful, painstaking labour in culling them for our reading pleasure.

— DI BRANDT
Windsor, Ontario
August 1998

"A poem is an archive for our times": Selecting and Editing Dorothy Livesay

Above all
a poem records speech:
the way it was said
between people   animals   birds
a poem is an archive for our times
          —Dorothy Livesay, "Anything Goes" (1983)

The archival history of Dorothy Livesay's previously unpublished and uncollected poems is documented not only in manuscripts and typescripts and periodicals, but also in her collections of poetry. Beginning in the late fifties, Livesay would repeatedly turn to her archive of unused poems as a source for her retrospective collections: *Selected Poems of Dorothy Livesay 1926-1956* (1957), *The Documentaries: Selected Longer Poems* (1968), *Collected Poems: The Two Seasons of Dorothy Livesay* (1972), *The Woman I Am* (1977; rpt. 1991), *Right Hand Left Hand: A True Life of the Thirties* (1977), *The Phases of Love* (1983), and *The Self-Completing Tree: Selected Poems* (1986). Of her twenty-one collections of poetry, seven are retrospectives—only two of seven collections in the fifties and the sixties, but five of ten in the seventies and eighties. Livesay is by no means unique in publishing retrospective collections in the prime and at the end of her career, but her unabated return to her archive is distinctive. *Archive for Our Times* merely extends Livesay's own practice of selective recovery from her unpublished and uncollected *oeuvre*.

In the foreword to her *Collected Poems*, Livesay reflects on the archival strata of her most comprehensive retrospective volume:

Because publishing poetry in Canada during the thirties, forties and fifties was nothing like what it became in the sixties—a bonanza!—my books that surfaced had layers of poems beneath them which were forced to remain submarine. For this reason I have arranged the unpublished poems as if they were in books on their own, with individual titles.[4]

Beneath these discrete sections of unpublished poems—by which Livesay must mean "unpublished in book form," since she includes previously uncollected poems from periodicals—are the deeper strata of unpublished and uncollected poems salvaged and displayed in these pages. There are still more poems, however, that "remain submarine." *Archive for Our Times* is a kind of archaeological exhibition, a showcase of poems extracted from layers of manuscripts and typescripts, newspapers and magazines, pamphlets and broadsheets. The proper context for this collection, then, is to resituate the layers of these previously uncollected and unpublished poems in and among the layers of her collected poems. This contextual approach imbricates several histories: Livesay's writing history, her publishing history, her personal/professional history, and the history of her archive.

In the process of writing the poems for her first chapbook, *Green Pitcher* (1928), and her first book, *Signpost* (1932), Livesay filled two notebooks, entitled "A Book of Rhymes Rhythms and Riots."[5] Written over a period of five years (1926-31), the three hundred and seventy-six pages of poetry contained in these notebooks could complete a collection by themselves. These notebooks exist alongside folders of loose manuscripts and typescripts from the same period. While attending Trinity College at the University of Toronto (1927-29, 1931) and during her year of study abroad in Aix-en-Provence (1929-30), Livesay published her poetry in student periodicals (*The Varsity, The Privateer*, and *St. Hilda's Chronicle*), in magazines (*Chatelaine, Saturday Night*, and *The Canadian Forum*), and in newspapers (*Vancouver Province*). Although this is an extremely prolific period

---

4   Dorothy Livesay, "Foreword," *Collected Poems: The Two Seasons of Dorothy Livesay* (Toronto: McGraw-Hill Ryerson, 1972) v.

5   Box 1, The Dorothy Livesay Holdings, Bruce Peel Special Collections Library, University of Alberta.

for Livesay (often penning several poems in a single day), it is also a period of poetic experimentation and inconsistency. That Livesay herself respected her readers' desire for quality over quantity of juvenilia is reflected in her recovery of only forty-three unpublished and uncollected poems from this period for "The Garden of Childhood," "Findings," and "The Garden of Love" sections of *Collected Poems*, and her retrieval of only twelve such poems for the "Adolescence" section of *The Phases of Love*. The twenty-seven poems from 1926 to 1932 selected for *Archive for Our Times* are not mere adolescent curios, but sources of Livesay's poetic self. Her formal repertoire is, even in these early poems, impressively variegated: Imagist free verse, haiku, blank verse sonnet, dialogue, dramatic monologue, even documentary. In terms of subject, these early poems frame portraits of bourgeois life: dog, gardener, pair of shoes, priest, blind man, thief, friend, butcher, baker, candlestickmaker, poet, woman, feminist, grandfathers, city, reader, Lazarus, and lovers. Even before her proletarian verse in the thirties, then, Livesay had started composing preliminary "poems for people."

After she obtained a *Diplôme d'Etudes Superieurs* from the Sorbonne for her thesis "Symbolism and the Metaphysical Tradition in Modern English Poetry" in 1932, Livesay entered the School of Social Work at the University of Toronto and was granted her diploma in 1934. While completing her field work in Montreal in 1933, and while employed as a case worker in Englewood, NJ, from 1934 to 1935, and in Vancouver, from 1936 to 1939, Livesay experienced a social landscape of unemployment, poverty, and racism that she documented in her proletarian verse. Having joined the Communist Party in 1933, Livesay also encountered a left-wing political landscape of United Front groups—including labour unions, the League Against War and Fascism, and the Youth Movement for Peace—whose activism infiltrated her poetry. Her involvement with the Progressive Arts Club (PAC), their agitation-propaganda ("agit-prop") theatre, and their two periodicals—*Masses* (1932-33) and *New Frontier: A Canadian Monthly Magazine of Literature and Social Criticism* (1936-37)—provided the communist-socialist arts communities in Toronto and Vancouver in which Livesay became politically and socially active. While engaged in social work in Toronto and Montreal, Livesay wrote poetry and reviews for *Masses*, and, while travelling west to Vancouver, worked as regional editor for *New Frontier*, giving talks about the magazine, soliciting subscriptions, and contributing poetry, reviews, and articles. For obvious reasons, then, the upheaval in Livesay's poetic sensibility—in the early thirties—was radical.

In the present collection, the initial break between the voices of Livesay's lyric and political poetry can be seen in the transition from "Yesterday's Children: A Cycle of Love Poems" (1931-32) to "Broadcast from Berlin" (1933). Poems from 1934 and thereafter, however, often merge her lyric and political voices: these voices overlap most prominently here in "Testament" (1934), "At the Beach," "In Praise of Evening," "New Day" (1937), "The Anarchist," "Spain" (1938), and "We Are Alone" (1939). Although she had renounced what she considered to be "bourgeois" and "decadent" forms of modern lyric poetry, Livesay had not abandoned but transformed the lyric.[6] For Livesay, the lyric had evolved into what she would later call the "documentary"—that is, poetry "based on topical data but held together by descriptive, lyrical, and didactic elements."[7] As Livesay herself has often said in interviews and autobiographical essays, her poems from the mid- to late thirties predominantly mediate between three strains of poetic influence: the modernist poetry of T. S. Eliot, Ezra Pound, Aldous Huxley, and the Sitwells that she studied at the Sorbonne; the Spanish Civil War poetry of W. H. Auden, Stephen Spender, and C. Day Lewis that she discovered in a Greenwich Village bookshop in 1933; and the agit-prop plays, mass chants, and proletarian verse that she encountered as a member of the PAC.

In contrast to her prolific period prior to 1932, Livesay's preoccupation with political activism and social work would lead to a sharp decline in her poetic output. As Lee Briscoe Thompson reports on her archival findings:

> After having produced an average of nearly one hundred poems every year from 1926 through 1931, [Livesay] drafted a total of

---

6   See Dorothy Livesay, "Decadence in Modern Bourgeois Poetry," *Right Hand Left Hand* (Erin, ON: Press Porcépic, 1977) 61-67. Originally a radio talk given on CBC Radio in 1936.

7   Dorothy Livesay, "The Documentary Poem: A Canadian Genre," *Contexts of Canadian Criticism: A Collection of Critical Essays*, ed. Eli Mandel, rev. ed. (Chicago: University of Chicago P, 1977) 269.

barely two dozen poems in the pre-New Jersey phase of 1932, 1933, and 1934. . . . Only four of her poems made it into print in those years, the depths of the Depression, and all in the Marxist periodical *Masses.* . . .[8]

Thompson then extends her analysis to Livesay's periodical publications throughout the decade:

Livesay had published almost exclusively in journals of limited and educated readership such as the *Canadian Poetry Magazine*, the *Canadian Forum*, the *Canadian Bookman*, *Masses*, and *New Frontier.* Of twenty-three social poems that she published during the 1930s, only three appeared in popular venues such as *Saturday Night* or the Vancouver *Province*, all at a very late stage of the decade, from March 1938 through November 1939, when even poetasters were trying their hand at a little social commentary.[9]

For instance, when Livesay's previously uncollected poems "Grouse Mountain" (1938) and "Words for a Chorus" (1939) appeared in *Full Tide*, a magazine of poetry written and published by the Vancouver Poetry Society, her milieu (including her husband, Duncan Macnair, a society executive at the time) abounded with such *dilettante* proletarian poets. In the late thirties, Livesay still maintained ties to the PAC writers who met at the West End Community Centre in Vancouver, and her poetry continued to speak to and for the PAC; but when *New Frontier* folded in 1937, Livesay had lost a key eastern outlet for her proletarian verse.

With the exception of "Seven Poems," "The Outrider," "Lorca," and the title poem from *Day and Night*, Livesay's political and proletarian verse from the thirties would disappear until *Collected Poems* and *Right Hand Left Hand* emerged in the seventies. Thompson offers some explanation for the disappearance and reappearance of Livesay's poetry from the thirties:

---

8   Lee Briscoe Thompson, *Dorothy Livesay*, Twayne's World Authors Ser. 784 (Boston: Twayne, 1987) 34-35.

9   Thompson 37.

The section of *Collected Poems* entitled "The Thirties" presents seventeen poems or poem "suites" almost exclusively on social and political themes. While five had appeared in whole or in part in primarily leftist journals, none had survived the winnowing for Livesay's 1957 *Selected Poems*, a suppression unsurprising in the face of the social apathy of the 1950s. In her 1972 *Collected Poems* Livesay was addressing recent veterans of the dynamic, protest-oriented 1960s and could feel assured at last of a receptive audience.[10]

What the foregoing passes over, however, is the spare representation of Livesay's thirties' poetry in *Day and Night* (1944) and *Poems for People* (1947). Only her title poem and one of her "Seven Poems" from *Day and Night* were actually published in the thirties.[11] Even though the title of *Poems for People* echoes the kind of proletarian verse Livesay had written in the Depression and Spanish Civil War years, these poems were neither written in the thirties nor promote the same party line. *Poems for People* represents a revision of Livesay's earlier social vision: it signals her poetic process of natural selection, her evolution from communist idealism in the thirties to social realism in the forties. Those poems from the forties that resurface in *Archive for Our Times* reflect her new " 'soft socialist' "[12] focus: personalized documentaries in "Hands" (1941) and "Motif for a Mural" (c. early 1940s), and home front commentaries in "The Take-Off," "Invasion," "Letter from Home" (1944), and "London in Retrospect" (1948).

Livesay was first awarded the Governor-General's Award for *Day and Night* in 1944 and again for *Poems for People* in 1947; also in 1947, she received the Lorne Pierce Gold Medal of the Royal Society of Canada. But even as her awards accumulated, Livesay's poetic production in the forties streamlined: only eighteen of forty-eight poems (and/or sequences) published in forties' periodicals remained uncol-

---

10   Thompson 40.

11   "The Fallow Mind," *Canadian Forum* (Dec. 1936): 71; rpt. in *Canadian Forum* (Dec. 1939) 277; rpt. in *Day and Night*, "Seven Poems [v. The fallow mind in winter . . .]" (Toronto: Ryerson, 1944) 5. "Day and Night," *Day and Night* 16-21.

12   Thompson 61.

lected by the time *Call My People Home* appeared in 1950; only ten of the uncollected eighteen have been passed over altogether (five of which appear here); and only twenty-six poems have never been published (seven of which appear here). Having so curtailed writing poetry, Livesay divested her creative energies in new directions: as a founding editor for the poetry magazine *Contemporary Verse* (1941-52); as a regional (west coast) editor for the literary magazine *Northern Review* (1945-47); as a European reporter for the *Toronto Star* (1946); as a free-lance journalist and script writer for CBC Radio (1947-53); and as editor of *The Collected Poems of Raymond Knister* (1949). Not surprisingly then, the number of poems from the forties dwarfs in comparison to the twenties and thirties. Even so, Livesay has since suppressed more than half of *Poems for People* from her retrospective collections. Unlike *Day and Night*, "far fewer verses in *Poems for People* have since been chosen to appear in the *Selected Poems* of 1957 and/or the *Collected Poems* of 1972: fourteen of the twenty-four have been passed over on one or both occasions ... [and] all but three of the poems so spurned were private, domestic, lyrical, anecdotal, or elegiac, not concerned with social commentary."[13] In *Archive for Our Times*, such poems as "Boy" (1943), "Of Love" (1944), "Sea Sequence" (1948), and "The Mirror" (c. 1949) exhibit those aspects of her poetry from the forties "not concerned with social commentary." As well, her meditations on art in "Variations on a Theme by Thomas Hardy" (1944) and "For Paul Robeson: Playing Othello" (1945) anticipate her renewed spiritual and aesthetic vision in the shorter lyrics of *Call My People Home* (1948-50) and the "Faces of Emily (1948-1953)" section of *Collected Poems*.

After publishing two chapbooks in the fifties, *Call My People Home* (1950) and *New Poems* (1955), Livesay would make the first delve into her archive of uncollected and unpublished poems in *Selected Poems of Dorothy Livesay 1926-1956* (1957). As an elaboration on the original title *Signature*,[14] the prosaic published title spells out Livesay's practice of revisionary selection: these *selected* poems are, if you will, her

---

13 Thompson 60.
14 See the original typescript for *Selected Poems* in Box 7, The Dorothy Livesay Holdings, Bruce Peel Special Collections Library, University of Alberta.

signature poems. *Selected Poems* bears Livesay's distinctive mark, that is, her signature of revisionary selection. Not restricting herself to poems from earlier collections, Livesay also selected previously unpublished and uncollected poems from the twenties, thirties, and forties, as well as new poems from the fifties. Among those new poems from the fifties suppressed from *Selected Poems* but now resurfaced, "Life of the Mind" (1951) is one of Livesay's signature poems in *Archive for Our Times*. Initially named "Lines on a Poet Who Stopped Writing,"[15] "Life of the Mind" concerns the poet's mental journeys to dislodge herself from a condition of silence. Interestingly, the motif of silence in "Life of the Mind" is ironic for several reasons: Livesay never actually stopped writing in the early fifties; she never selected "Life of the Mind" for any of her collections; and when she submitted the poem to *Northern Review*, John Sutherland returned it with a rejection letter.[16] In retrospect, the motif of silence is the distinctive mark of Livesay's uncollected and unpublished poetry: every poem selected for *Archive for Our Times* was once silenced in the process of selection for previous collections; every selection leaves behind an indelible signature of silence.

In addition to publishing three collections of poetry, the fifties also witness Livesay's entry into educational work and return to social work: from 1951 to 1953, Livesay taught creative writing at the

---

15   Box 4, The Dorothy Livesay Holdings, Bruce Peel Special Collections Library, University of Alberta. On her worksheet, Livesay has written P.K. Page in parentheses below the original title. The attribution of such a poem to Page is certainly premature (or at least anachronistic), given that Page would publish her Governor-General's Award-winning collection *The Metal and the Flower* in 1954. The parenthetical reference to Page disappears in the subsequent typescripts.

16   See Sutherland's letter to Livesay, dated March 8, 1951, in *The Letters of John Sutherland, 1942-1956*, ed. Bruce Whiteman (Toronto: ECW, 1992) 181-82. Livesay submitted both "Life of the Mind" and "Ancestral Theme" (the original title of her frontispiece to *Selected Poems*, later retitled "Signature"). Sutherland rejected both poems. Given that she included "Signature" but not "Life of the Mind" in *Selected Poems*, the ironic silencing of the latter is perpetuated not only by Sutherland but also by Livesay herself.

University of British Columbia; from 1953 to 1955, she worked as program director of the Young Adult Department at the Vancouver YMCA; and, from 1956 to 1958, she studied for her Diploma in Secondary Level Teaching of English. Her four-part sequence printed here, "Academicals" (1955-56), mockingly documents her return to academia. Many poems she wrote while researching creative methods of teaching English at the Institute of Education, University of London (1958-59) and while working as a program assistant for the Department of Education at UNESCO in Paris (1959-60) have already been selected for the "Poems from Exile (1958-1959)" section of her *Collected Poems*; here, other poems written in England ("Guy Fawkes," "Walking to Work: London, 1958," "Spring in Russell Square," and "Letter to My Daughter") and in France ("Côte d'Azur," "The Gift," "Paysage Provençale," and "Sunflowers") revisit those European locales to which the poet makes imagined journeys in "Life of the Mind."

Throughout the fifties, however, a kind of silence not envisioned in "Life of the Mind" would haunt Livesay: first her father, John Frederick Bligh Livesay, died on June 15, 1944; her mother, Florence Hamilton Randal Livesay, died on July 28, 1953; then her husband, Duncan Cameron Macnair, died on February 12, 1959. One of her best-known poems from this period, "Lament," an elegy for her father, was first published in 1953 (and later included in *Selected Poems, Collected Poems, The Woman I Am*, and *The Self-Completing Tree*). Contemporary poems collected and published here for the first time offer different elegiac perspectives: "Loss" (1956), "The Immortals" (1957), "Words for Our Time" (1959), and "In the Ward" (1959). Like her "Poems from Exile" section of *Collected Poems*, one of Livesay's poems from 1959 that appears here, "Man on Grouse Mountain," commemorates both the spirit and the ideas of her late husband.[17] Livesay's years of exile and of mourning in the late fifties were neither years of alienation nor of silence; rather, the majority of her poems from the fifties were written from 1958 to 1959.

---

17 See Box 4, File 7 in The Dorothy Livesay Holdings, Bruce Peel Special Collections Library, University of Alberta. On her worksheets, Livesay dedicated "Man on Grouse Mountain" to D.C.M. (Duncan Cameron Macnair). The dedication was later dropped from the typescript.

From 1960 to 1963, Livesay was appointed as a specialist in teacher training in Northern Rhodesia (present-day Zambia) at Chalimbana Teachers' College. In contrast to her prolific period of exile in the late fifties, during these four years in Africa, Livesay composed only sixteen poems.[18] After her return to Canada in 1963, her first suite of Africa poems was published as a pamphlet, *The Colour of God's Face* (1964), later revised and published as the "Zambia" suite in *The Unquiet Bed* (1967). Another suite not included in *The Unquiet Bed*, "The Second Language," appeared in the "To Speak with Tongues (1960-1964)" section of *Collected Poems*. Such previously unpublished poems as "Benny Lighting a Fire," "The Child on Steps" (1963), "The colour of your talking . . ." (1965), and "Hibiscus" (1969), as well as such previously uncollected poems as "Cockcrow" and "Africa" (1965), complement Livesay's longer, previously collected African suites. Included here, her long poem "The Hammer and the Shield" (1966) signifies yet another revisionary turn in Livesay's poetics—that is, her return in the sixties to the documentary poems of the thirties and early forties. Similar in form to the six long poems selected for her retrospective 1968 collection *The Documentaries: Selected Longer Poems*, "The Hammer and the Shield" is an historical documentary of Livesay's experience of topical events in Africa. In what she subtitles "A Found Poem" (a variant of the documentary poem), the "objective facts" and the documentary materials about her historical subject, former United Nations' Secretary-General Dag Hammarskjöld, are mounted in dialectical relation to "the subjective feelings of the poet."[19] A complex montage of Livesay's African

---

18   Thompson 92.
19   Livesay, "The Documentary Poem" 269. The documentary materials
     Livesay has "found" include: poems and diary entries from Dag
     Hammarskjöld, *Markings*, trans. Leif Sjöberg and W.H. Auden, intro. by
     W.H. Auden (London: Faber, 1964); excerpts from Dag Hammarskjöld,
     *Servant of Peace: A Selection of the Speeches and Statements of Dag
     Hamnmarskjöld,* ed. and intro. by Wilder Foote (New York and Evanston:
     Harper, 1962); excerpts from U.N. records now collected in the *Public
     Papers of the Secretaries-General of the United Nations,* vol. 5, ed. Andrew
     W. Cordier and Wilder Foote (New York and London: Columbia UP,
     1975); and excerpts from a lecture by Julius K. Nyevere, "The Courage of

experience and of African history, "The Hammer and the Shield" is another of her poems that was, even in the publishing boom of the sixties, "forced to remain submarine."

After her return to Vancouver in the summer of 1963, Livesay began graduate study at the University of British Columbia; she completed her thesis, "Sound and Rhythm in Contemporary Canadian Poetry," and received her Masters of Education in 1966. Active in various pedagogical roles throughout the sixties, she worked as a lecturer in poetry in the Department of Creative Writing at the University of British Columbia, from 1965 to 1966, and later took a position as writer-in-residence at the University of New Brunswick from 1966 to 1968. Into the seventies, she held positions at the University of Alberta, as an associate professor of English, from 1968 to 1971; at the University of Victoria, as a visiting lecturer in English, from 1972 to 1974; and at the University of Manitoba, as a writer-in-residence and professor of English, from 1974 to 1976. After returning to British Columbia in the late seventies, she took positions at Simon Fraser University, as a writer-in-residence, from 1980 to 1981, and as a creative writing instructor, from 1981 to 1982; after a fifty-two year hiatus, she returned to the University of Toronto, where she was installed at New College, as a writer-in-residence, from 1983 to 1984. Drawing upon her two decades of pedagogical experience, Livesay commenced in the sixties and continued through the eighties to reflect upon younger generations of poets and critics whom she encountered in cities across Canada. Many of the poems first published and collected here—"At Birney's," "POEMSNAPS" (1967), "McLuhan Criticized," "On Cleaning a Chicken," "Interior Landscape" (1971), "The Interrogation" (1974), "Iconoclast" (1976), "Ars Poetica," "Caution: To Nadine" (1977), "The Continuum," "The Critics" (1978), and "Epiphany" (1983)—offer Livesay's contempo-

---

Reconciliation," *The Quest for Peace: The Dag Hammarskjöld Memorial Lectures,* ed. Andrew W. Cordier and Wilder Foote (New York and London: Columbia UP, 1965) 9-28. Livesay has introduced poetic line breaks into many of the "found" prose documents; these line breaks I have maintained, but have restored the original line breaks to the quoted poems. I have set all of Livesay's quotations in italics, if not already in quotation marks.

rary and revisionary insights into literary communities and critics and poets of her times.

Livesay's cross-country travels in the sixties and seventies would also introduce her to a series of regional small press publishers and periodicals. For instance, "Post-Operative Instructions" (1968), included here, was first printed by Quarry Press in Kingston as a broadside; *Disasters of the Sun* (1971), included in *Collected Poems*, was first published by Blackfish Press in Burnaby as a "broadside folio." Although she had started publishing poems in the Fredericton-based magazine *The Fiddlehead* in 1953 (notably, after the demise of the Vancouver-based magazine *Contemporary Verse*), Livesay's increased appearances in other maritime periodicals (*The Atlantic Advocate*, *Steamer*) corresponded with her residency in Fredericton.[20] Published in Fred Cogswell's series of Fiddlehead Poetry Books, the first edition of Livesay's chapbook *Plainsongs* (1968) punctuated her tenure at Fredericton; the revised and expanded edition (1971) included new poems in the section "Living" that document not only her recent move to Edmonton but also her lifetime of living on the move. Now published in *Archive for Our Times*, poems such as "View North," "It's Time" (1965), "The Elms," "Côte d'Azur" (1966), "Aliens All" (1967), "Ceremonial Journey," "Water Colours: Victoria," "High Rise" (1969), and "The Invasion" (1971) also record her frequent global migrations and her enduring sense of place in a manner consonant with both *Plainsongs* and *The Unquiet Bed*.

Even as she selected her longer poems for *The Documentaries* in 1968, revised and expanded *Plainsongs* in 1971, and prepared the typescripts for her retrospective *Collected Poems* in 1972, Livesay revisited some of her unpublished poems originally written in the fifties—"Ceremonial Journey" (1953), "Water Colours: Victoria" (1956), and "Sonnet for the Times" (1958)—and then revised them in 1969. These revised poems, now published here, may have been considered for *Plainsongs* or even for *Collected Poems*. Livesay's revisionary practice exercised in these poems encapsulates, in a small way,

---

20 See the following previously uncollected poems, included here: "Sky Watchers," "Statues" (1966), "Fundy" (1967), "A Threnody: Easter, 1968" (1968), "Among Friends," and "Carman and His Editors" (1969).

the return to her archive of unpublished and uncollected poems that led to the publication of *Collected Poems*.

While she attended to *Collected Poems,* Livesay also turned her attention to editing two anthologies of women's poetry—*40 Women Poets of Canada* (1971) and *Woman's Eye: 12 B.C. Poets* (1974).Conceived as a reaction to the paucity of women represented in anthologies of Canadian poetry, *40 Women Poets of Canada* attempted to shift the balance of what Livesay perceived to be a male-centred Canadian canon exclusively constructed by male editors. In bringing together established and upcoming poets in both anthologies, Livesay created a bridge between contemporary women poets of her past and of her present. As well, the explicit feminist intention behind the two anthologies coincided with the rising interests of feminist literary critics who have since held Livesay's woman-centred poetry in high esteem. Indeed, the Dorothy Livesay special issue of *Room of One's Own* (1979) represented both Livesay's and her critics' feminist concerns in the seventies. Nearly all of the poems Livesay contributed to the issue were collected in the "Voices of Women" section of *The Phases of Love* (1983); together with the "Adolecence" section of poetry from the twenties and thirties, Livesay's commitment to writing for and about women in this late volume extends over six decades. Women's issues raised in such poems from the seventies and early eighties as "Out of the cradle . . ." (1970), "Three Kingdoms" (1975), "Martyrs, Anonymous" (1979), "The Woman Syndrome," "To Robbie Burns" (c. 1970s), and "Jove's Daughter" (1981), open Livesay's woman's eye into even wider focus in *Archive for Our Times*.

After *Collected Poems*, Livesay produced two collections of new poems: one chapbook, *Nine Poems of Farewell* 1972-73 (1973; rpt. 1976), and one book, *Ice Age* (1975)—both by small press publishers, Black Moss Press in Coatsworth, ON and Press Porcépic in Erin, ON, respectively. Expressions of loss, mourning, aging, and decay that appear in *Nine Poems* and *Ice Age* resonate with poems from the sixties and seventies included in the present collection: "Widow," "Statues" (1966), "Persephone" (1967), "Birthday," "Woman" (1968), "Savour of Salt" (1971), "Retirement in Victoria" (1974), "Canadian" (1978), "I Keep Preparing," and "In the Cupboard" (1979). In counterpoint, expressions of sexuality, desire, and rejuvenation arise here in "Between a Thousand" (1967-68), "Imprints," "Leda Again" (1969), "Flight 403" (1971), "Annunciation" (1974), "Time Zone" (1976), "Comrade" (1977), "Rush Hour" (1978), "A Stranger   But

No Ghost," and "Roomers" (c. 1970s). In combination, these later poems articulate the contradictions and complexities of coming to completion in life and in death.

During her residence at the University of Manitoba in the mid-seventies, Livesay founded, funded, and edited the journal *CV/II*, so named in memory of the forties' magazine *Contemporary Verse*. These years in Winnipeg culminated in the publication of two retrospective collections and in receiving the Queen's Canada Medal—all in 1977. Assisted by Dennis Cooley and Nadine McInnis, Livesay selected the poems for *The Woman I Am* (1977), and, together with her editors David Arnason and Kim Todd, Livesay compiled her multigenre documentary of the thirties, *Right Hand Left Hand* (1977). In calling attention to the coincident publication of *The Woman I Am* and *Right Hand Left Hand*, both by Press Porcépic, as well as the prior publication of *Collected Poems*, Thompson notes the disparities between and complementarities of these retrospective collections from the seventies:

> When in 1977 Livesay published a selection of her work under the title *The Woman I Am*, it was in one respect noticeably different from the *Collected Poems* of five years previous. True, as a "selected" rather than a "collected," it could not possibly aspire to the completeness of its predecessor, nor was there space to provide so elaborate a chronological or thematic structure to the volume. But the significant difference lay elsewhere. The *Collected Poems* had taken pains to bring to the surface nearly two dozen "submarine" social poems of a period dear to Livesay's heart: the 1930s. *The Woman I Am*, by contrast, severely ignored all of her social poetry of the 1930s. . . . [But] [i]t is worth remembering as well that 1977 saw the publication of not only *The Woman I Am* but also *Right Hand Left Hand*, a book dedicated entirely to the 1930s. . . .[21]

Extending into the twenty years since her *Selected Poems* in 1957, *The Woman I Am* represents a selection from 1926 to 1977, but unevenly so: Livesay "allowed only thirty-three selections to come from the

---

21   Thompson 67-68.

first forty-five years; thirty-nine poems date from the seven years thereafter, several seeing print for the first time."[22] While she may have passed over her social verse from the thirties and forties for the opening section, "1926-1971," Livesay's selection for the final section, "1975-1977," addresses contemporaneous issues of social and political concern. Indicative of recent directions Livesay's poetry had taken, *The Woman I Am* exchanges one era of social and political verse from the past (1932-1947) for one of the present (1975-1977). Always conscious of the poet's political and social responsibilities, Livesay never failed in the sixties and seventies to draft poems in response to her contemporary activist audience, including those collected and published in *Archive for Our Times*: "Sonnet for the Times" (1969), "Jack on the Telephone Beanstalk" (1970), "Not" (1972), "Barometer Falling" (1974), "Gabe," "The Bethune Wind," "I, Happiest" (1976), and "All the Good Things" (1978).

Livesay's first collection in the eighties, *The Raw Edges: Voices from Our Time* (1981), published in Winnipeg by Turnstone Press, stages an apocalyptic, anti-nuclear cast of protest poetry. *The Raw Edges* is arranged for multiple voices, in a manner reminiscent of her agit-prop plays from the thirties and her documentaries from the thirties, forties, fifties, and sixties. The arrangement also typifies Livesay's tendency to create discrete poems, then later revise and integrate them into longer lyric sequences. In fact, many of the poems in *The Raw Edges* exist as individual poems in manuscripts and typescripts from the early eighties. This revisionary practice of taking individual poems, cropping their titles, and arranging them into longer units is common among Livesay's collections from the forties and thereafter.[23] Likewise, the "Adolescence" and "Fire and Frost" sections of

---

22   Thompson 11.

23   Some earlier examples include: "Seven Poems" and "Five Poems" in *Day and Night*; "Zambia" in *The Unquiet Bed*; "The Pied Piper of Edmonton" in *Plainsongs*; "The Garden of Love," "Queen City," "Depression Suite," "In Time of War," "Prophet of the New World," and "A Ballet of Squares" in *Collected Poems*. As well, see "Yesterday's Children: A Cycle of Love Poems" (1931-32) and "Water Colours: Victoria" (1969) in the present volume. Many of the poems from "Yesterday's Children" were previously selected for "The Garden of Love" section of *Collected Poems*.

The Phases of Love (1983) integrate previously unpublished poems into longer lyric suites. As well, *Feeling the Worlds: New Poems* (1984) is arranged into four suites of titled poems, though Livesay's revisionary practice is not so prominent there. Her subtitle is somewhat misleading, however, even hiding what is another visitation of her archive: some of the pieces for this 1984 collection of "new poems" were first published in periodicals dating back to the late sixties and early seventies, and one was reprinted from *Ice Age*. Even for her penultimate collection of "new poems," then, Livesay would mine the ever-renewable resources of her archive.

Although she closed *Feeling the Worlds* with the poem "Epitaph," the selection of poems from the eighties represented in *Archive for Our Times* resists such a trope of closure. Poems such as "Old Woman," "Willow Island (Lake Winnipeg)," "Pause," and "The Tipster" (1980) envision rebirth, and others like "The Still World," "Self on TV" (1980), "Epiphany," and "Anything Goes" (1983) imagine strategies of survival. In fact, in a rare 1991 chapbook entitled *Awakenings*, published by Reference West in Victoria, Livesay resurrected herself for a series of fifteen sparely written new poems.

In *The Self-Completing Tree: Selected Poems* (1986), Livesay would perform another act of self-regeneration by yet again returning to her archive of previously collected, uncollected, and unpublished poems. Where her title connotes the *completion* of her poetic self, her subtitle denotes the *selection* from her complete poetry: taken together, the full title signifies how Livesay's process of self-completion is qualified by her process of self-selection. So after selecting from previously published poems, supplementing these with previously uncollected and unpublished poems, and casting the whole into seven, thematically arranged sections, Livesay declares in her opening statement: "This is the selection of poems that I would like to be remembered by. Rather than being strictly chronological, it is wrapped around certain themes that I see recurring throughout the years."[24] *Archive for Our Times* does not follow Livesay's model of thematic arrangement, opting instead for chronological order: my process of selection, however, does maintain Livesay's vision of cer-

---

24   Dorothy Livesay, *The Self-Completing Tree: Selected Poems* (Toronto and Victoria: Press Porcépic, 1986) 3.

tain themes that surface throughout her *oeuvre* of published, unpublished, and uncollected poems. Indeed, one of Livesay's recurrent themes and practices is that of returning to her archive.

In so far sketching Livesay's personal and publication histories from 1926 to 1991, I have dotted an outline of her previously collected, unpublished, and uncollected poems. What remains to be considered, then, is the history of the actual archives from which Livesay's previously unpublished poems have been selected. As an unwieldy and unbound text, Livesay's archival papers are not something a reader can carry in a bag, read on the bus, or find space for on a bookshelf. *Archive for Our Times* is in part an abridged edition, so to speak, of the massive holdings of original manuscripts and typescripts deposited in archives at the University of Manitoba and the University of Alberta. Similar to the publication histories of her poetry collections and uncollected poems, Livesay's papers carry their own archival history, one which predates the depositing of her papers at archival institutions.

A partial history of Livesay's archive is documented in a series of letters, written to Livesay by her friend Elizabeth Varley. Hired by Livesay in the late sixties, Varley indexed Livesay's archive of manuscripts and typescripts and transcribed most of her manuscripts to typescript. The initial gathering, sorting, and cataloguing stages of archival work were then initiated by Varley, but eventually abandoned. Livesay clearly hired Varley with the intention to recover and publish at least part of her corpus of unpublished and uncollected poems. In fact, Varley's inventory led to the recovery of many poems for Livesay's retrospective collections and revisionary practice in the seventies and eighties.

Varley's earliest extant correspondence with Livesay is a letter dated June 3, 1939, in which Varley recounts their work for the Vancouver branch of the Progressive Arts Club.[25] The Livesay-Varley correspondence does not recommence until October 9, 1968 when Varley, living in Sechelt, BC, writes to Livesay, living in Edmonton and teaching at the University of Alberta. The correspondence un-

---

25   All quotation and paraphrase of Varley's letters in this afterword refer to
      MSS 37, Box 73, File 17 in The Dorothy Livesay Papers, Department of
      Archives and Special Collections, Elizabeth Dafoe Library, University of
      Manitoba.

cannily picks up where it left off—insofar as Varley is now sorting through Livesay's papers from the time of the last letter in 1939. But the thirty-year hiatus has radically changed the nature of their relationship. And their relationship will change further as Varley becomes more familiar with Livesay's papers.

At the initial stage of sorting and identifying, Varley is a stranger to Livesay's papers, uncertain what to do with untitled and undated poems and how to read Livesay's handwriting. Varley's October 9, 1968 letter to Livesay perfectly describes my attempts to decipher Livesay's often illegible manuscripts and to ascertain dates for the previously unpublished poems:

> I have a whole pile of ones I cannot read at all, so I'll send them to you when I get a little further along. I mean, they have nothing but the lines to identify them, and I can't make out even the first lines. You would probably know at once what they are, and if published.

Varley still defers authority over the archive to Livesay, its creator, even though Livesay's authority is limited once Varley starts to reorganize the original order of the papers. Having access to Livesay, Varley assumes that the poet's memory will sufficiently serve as the supplemental archive to the material archive. While the poems in Livesay's notebooks from the twenties and early thirties are usually dated to the day, and those undated are easily given approximate dates given their linear order of composition, the hundreds of undated poems written on torn sheets from notepads and typed on loose sheets of foolscap are more difficult for Livesay or Varley to date with any exactitude. Often either Livesay or Varley has written the year followed by a question mark on the originals; others have been dated approximately because Livesay has kept copies of poems submitted to periodicals, and these always have her various addresses at head of the page; still others have been dated according to first publication in periodicals. But one month into her archival work, Varley is nowhere near such a system. Overwhelmed by the sheer volume and disorganization of the papers, Varley writes to Livesay in her letter of November 8, 1968:

> I'm having a bad time with the huge bundle of loose stuff. No dates, and half of it with nothing to refer to to identify. . . . I'll come on a

typed sheet that looks familiar and find I have one the same in a back folder—perhaps '44, which I've not been able to identify. Then I find another among '52s. Then I may find the original in the big bundle I'm working on, deeper down—or part of it, and find the rest, or some more, at least, on different paper, later on, and with often origs. quite different to [sic] finished work, it[']s confusing and slow. I enjoy the little game, though, and make as good progress as I can. I haven't a photographic mind.

Varley's letters to Livesay represent to me a kind of kindred archivist's journal: they both help to explain editorial difficulties in dating Livesay's manuscripts and typescripts and to describe the process of archivization itself. They also represent the impossibility of ever knowing the original order of the papers, of playing the "little game" over which Varley agonized, learning the rules on the spot and finding that the rules changed as soon as she wrote them down.

Varley's letters further reveal the unavoidable desires of the archivist to stop indexing and start reading. In an undated letter, Varley additionally takes on the work of both editor and literary critic:

> I've taken time to read your poetry lately—sometimes because I have to, sometimes for enjoyment after I finish. I haven't looked at anything after the early fifties, but I find your best expression is from spontaneous emotional response to nature — including human nature . . . consciously perceived. And it's interesting to follow the development of some of your poems, from first draft to finished poem. . . . Please excuse my presumsion [sic] in making literary remarks.

What Varley exposes here is the division of labour between archivist, editor, and literary critic: her job as archivist is to catalogue the poems, but she is not to interpret them. She is conscious of her breach of the archivist's contract to remain disinterested, objective, impartial. Yet she is merely exercising her new-found authority as custodian and interpreter of the archive: the meaning of archive, as Jacques Derrida reminds us, comes from the Greek *arkheion*,

> initially a house, a domicile, an address, the residence of the superior magistrates, the *archons*, those who commanded. . . . The archons are first of all the documents' guardians. . . . They

are also accorded hermeneutic right and competence. They have the power to interpret the archives.[26]

Varley has taken residence in the archive; but she questions her right and power to interpret Livesay's papers—though not as an archivist, but as a literary critic. Ever since Varley cut short her "literary remarks" on Livesay's papers, commentary on her unpublished poems has been limited to select archivists, archival researchers, and literary critics. Although mediated by my editorial act of selection, the present volume accords a wider audience access and power to interpret Livesay's archive.

As an amateur archivist, Varley expresses fears that her work is haphazard and unprofessional in her letter of December 5, 1968: "Practically no dates after the thirties. I group by guess & by publications, which are sometimes very vague." Even after personal consultation with Livesay on the catalogue of poems, Varley points out inaccuracies in Livesay's dating of poems in a letter of January 5, 1969:

> Everything will need to be recatalogued, for some poems are still wrongly dated—e.g. came on something you had dated a couple of years after it had been published! Fast work, that! No wonder: looking back over a life time at a thousand poems among the heap of ten thousand other written words. I found another couple poems of which you have no record here at all. . . .

Again, Varley demonstrates her right and competence to interpret the archive: Livesay's mind is not photographic either, and her memory archive is contradicted by Varley's reading of the material archive. And Varley is by no means exaggerating: Livesay's uncollected, unpublished, and unfinished poems *by themselves* amount to over a thousand discrete pieces, many in multiple drafts.

Livesay's letters to Varley have not been catalogued and preserved in an archive; hence this archival history of Livesay's papers is documented only in Varley's words. We may, however, deduce Livesay's intentions in having Varley catalogue her archive of poetry. That

---

26   Jacques Derrida, *Archive Fever: A Freudian Impression*, trans. Eric Prenowitz (Chicago: U of Chicago P, 1996) 2.

Livesay herself initiated the process of cataloging her archival papers in the late sixties helps to explain her recovery of previously unpublished and uncollected poems for her retrospective collections in the seventies and eighties. In an oral diary recorded on reel to reel in the early seventies, Livesay confesses her motives and desires to recover her uncollected and unpublished poems:

> Well, the thing is that it's high time I had a collected poems . . . there does seem to be a great response and interest in my work, and particularly in my work I did in the thirties. So call it foolish ambition, driving paranoia, call it what you like, I've been sufficiently reared in a literary atmosphere that I don't feel I can be silent. I feel the need to be published. Of course this is not modest, not a thing that leads to serenity. There seems to be ambition there, rivalry in my desire to be heard. Yet if I let it go, it nags and nags at me. I think to myself, this work done so long ago isn't any more mine. But it's something to do with the growth of this country. It needs to be known. Oh dear. Why do I have this drive? Why do I believe in my own work? I don't know. . . . I feel there's my lower self that is extremely ambitious and even malicious, and pernicious, that wants this kind of adulation. But there's another more rational self that still can't get away from the desire to have these things in print. . . .[27]

Livesay's renewed attention to her poetic history is clearly conflicted: she signs over her papers to the care of an archivist, she even dispossesses her poems, yet she still desires publication, recognition, and commemoration. This unresolved conflict is testified in an early version of her poem "Memo to My Daughter," dated 1967, just one year prior to Varley's arrival in Sechelt:

> Nothing is ever finished!
> I cannot clear up my papers

---

27 TC 31, Box 1, Tape 11 in The Dorothy Livesay Papers, Department of Archives and Special Collections, Elizabeth Dafoe Library, University of Manitoba.

for you to sort through.
When I go—
let them go too.

. . . .

The record of our life
is lived in secret
inside the head.
When someone forgets
to wind up the brain
it stops:
secrets are useless[28]

Livesay's archivization of her papers during the seventies ensures that "Nothing is ever finished." The question of the archive, Derrida says,

> is a question of the future, the question of the future itself, the question of a response, of a promise and of a responsibility for tomorrow. The archive: if we want to know what that will have meant, we will only know in times to come. Perhaps. Not tomorrow but in times to come, later on or perhaps never.[29]

In Derrida's notion of the archive, as a promise, and, in Livesay's poem, as an open secret, there is an ambivalence: the archive holds the promise that the record of our lives will never be finished, that our secret lives will be written in the future; or, perhaps, our "secrets are useless."

Even now, much of Livesay's archive is still held in secret: her archive of unpublished and uncollected poems is so vast that to publish all of the pieces would require multiple volumes. Approximately one quarter of Livesay's total uncollected and unpublished poems is represented here. In choosing from these poems in her papers and in periodicals, I have arranged an historically significant and representative sequence of Livesay's various poetic styles and

---

28 MSS 37, Box 82, File 9 in The Dorothy Livesay Papers, Department of Archives and Special Collections, Elizabeth Dafoe Library, University of Manitoba.

29 Derrida 36.

forms, as well as her social, political, and personal concerns, between 1926 and 1983. Hence the poems appear in chronological order, sequenced according to composition date (or an approximation) for unpublished poems and to publication date for uncollected poems. Unpublished poems for which only the year of composition is known appear after poems for which the month and/or date of composition is recorded. Unpublished poems for which only the decade of composition is known appear at the end of each section. Following an historical narrative, then, the selection and arrangement of poems recreates for Livesay's reader the effect of leafing through her archive. "A poem is an archive for our times" is a line taken from "Anything Goes," the latest of Livesay's unpublished poems collected here: it speaks both to the need for readers to regard these poems as a retrospection on Canadian literary culture from past times, and to see their representation as yet another revision of Livesay's poetic history for *our* times.

—DEAN J. IRVINE
Montreal
July 1998

EDITORIAL NOTES AND INDICES

Chronological Index of Archival and Periodical Sources

For previously unpublished poems, the manuscript (MS) or typescript (TS) source is indicated first, followed by the date (or, if no date [n.d.] is available, an approximation [*circa*.] is given). For previously uncollected poems, the periodical source and date appears (listed first in each entry, and, if extant and accurately dated, followed by the MS or TS source and date). With respect to previously unpublished poems, I have reconstructed the manuscript and/or typescript histories, following the trajectory of Livesay's revisions, and then adopted the latest or revised (rev.) MS or TS version as the copy text (listed first in each entry, and, if the copy text is undated or if earlier dated versions exist, followed by a supplemental MS or TS source and date). I have changed capitalization or added punctuation only in those previously unpublished poems in which the same is obviously present but inconsistently used. With previously uncollected poems, I have maintained the text as it appears in the periodical source, and amended only typographical and orthographical errors.

ANYTHING GOES: THE 1980S

Alphabetical Index of Poems

ALSO BY DOROTHY LIVESAY

Green Pitcher (Toronto: Macmillan, 1928).

Signpost (Toronto: Macmillan, 1932).

Day and Night (Toronto: Ryerson; Boston: Bruce Humphries, 1944).

Poems for People (Toronto: Ryerson, 1947).

Call My People Home (Toronto: Ryerson, 1950).

New Poems (Toronto: Emblem Books, 1955).

Selected Poems of Dorothy Livesay 1926-1956 (Toronto: Ryerson, 1957).

The Colour of God's Face (Vancouver: Unitarian Service Committee, 1964).

The Unquiet Bed, illus. Roy Kiyooka (Toronto: Ryerson, 1968).

The Documentaries: Selected Longer Poems (Toronto: Ryerson, 1968).

Plainsongs (Fredericton: Fiddlehead Poetry Books, 1969; rev. and enl. ed. Fredericton: Fiddlehead Poetry Books, 1971).

Disasters of the Sun (Burnaby, BC: Blackfish, 1971).

Collected Poems: The Two Seasons of Dorothy Livesay (Toronto and New York: McGraw-Hill Ryerson, 1972).

Nine Poems of Farewell 1972-1973 (Coatsworth, ON: Black Moss, 1973; rpt. 1976).

A Winnipeg Childhood (Winnipeg: Peguis, 1973); rpt. as *Beginnings: A Winnipeg Childhood* (Toronto: New Press, 1975); rev. ed. *Beginnings* (Winnipeg: Peguis, 1988).

Ice Age (Erin, ON: Press Porcépic, 1975).

The Woman I Am (Erin, ON: Press Porcépic, 1977; rev. ed. Montreal: Guernica, 1991).

Right Hand Left Hand: A True Life of the Thirties, eds. David Arnason and Kim Todd (Erin, ON: Press Porcépic, 1977).

The Raw Edges: Voices from Our Time (Winnipeg: Turnstone, 1981).

The Phases of Love (Toronto: Coach House, 1983).

Feeling the Worlds: New Poems (Fredericton: Goose Lane, 1984).

The Self-Completing Tree: Selected Poems (Toronto and Victoria: Press Porcépic, 1986).

Les Âges de l'amour, trans. Jean Antonin Billard (Montreal: Guernica, 1989).

The Husband (Charlottetown: Ragweed, 1990).

Awakenings (Victoria: Reference West, 1991).

Journey With My Selves: A Memoir 1909-1963 (Vancouver and Toronto: Douglas and McIntyre, 1991).

DEAN J. IRVINE has taken undergraduate and graduate degrees at the University of Victoria and the University of Calgary, and is currently a doctoral candidate in the Department of English at McGill University, where he is writing his thesis on Canadian women modernist poets and editors of little magazines from the thirties, forties, and fifties. His essays and reviews have appeared in *Canadian Literature*, *Essays on Canadian Writing*, *Beyond the Orchard: Essays on* The Martyrology, and *Ariel*, and will appear in forthcoming essay collections on the Canadian short story and on Malcolm Lowry. As well, he is a member of the editorial collective of *filling Station*, a Calgary-based magazine of contemporary writing.